ADULT COLORING BOOK
STRESS RELIEVING DESIGNS
ANIMLS ,MANDALAS

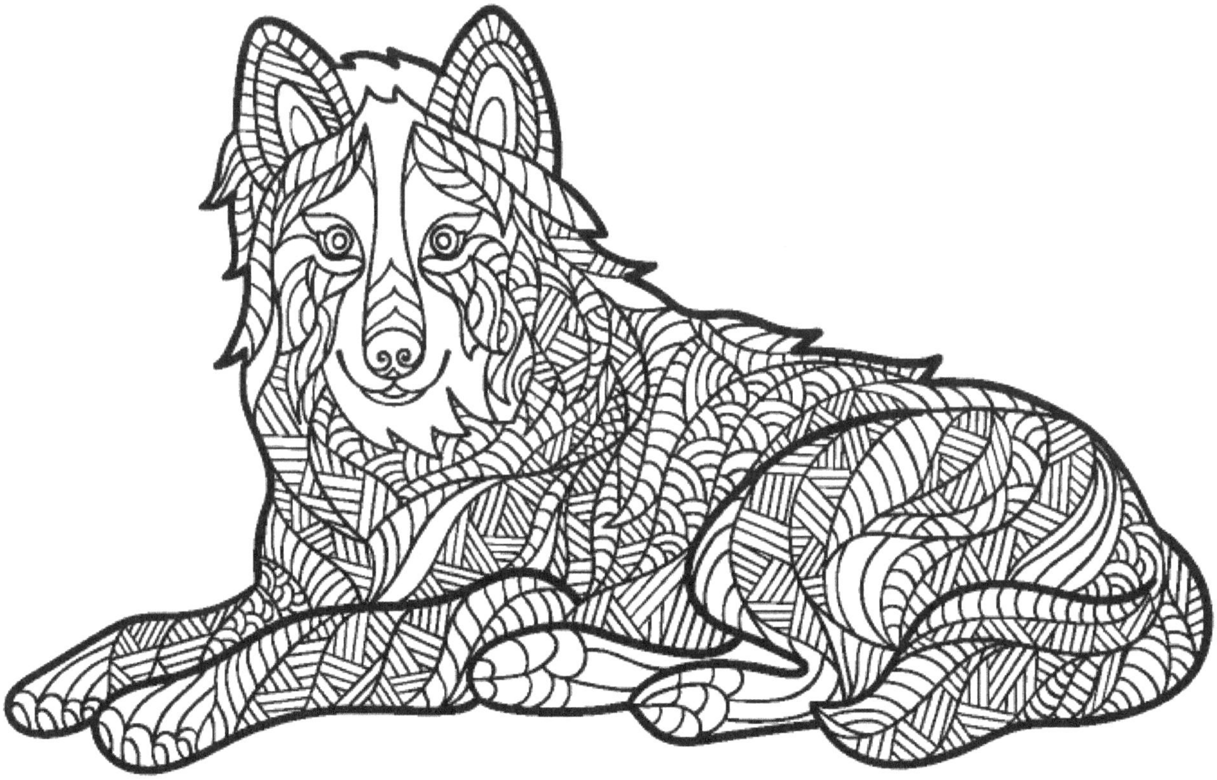

Copyright @ 2020 by Nana Emillie

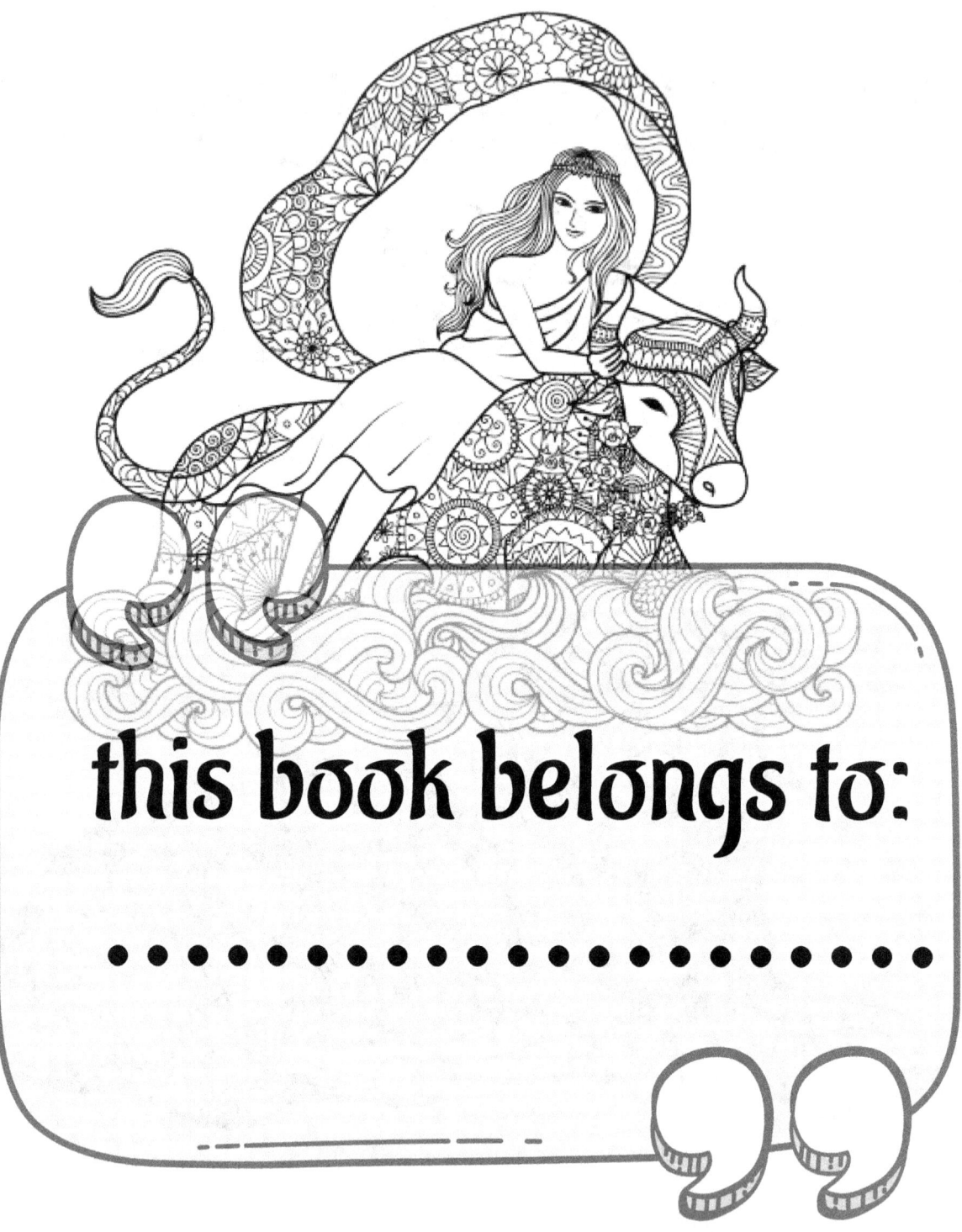

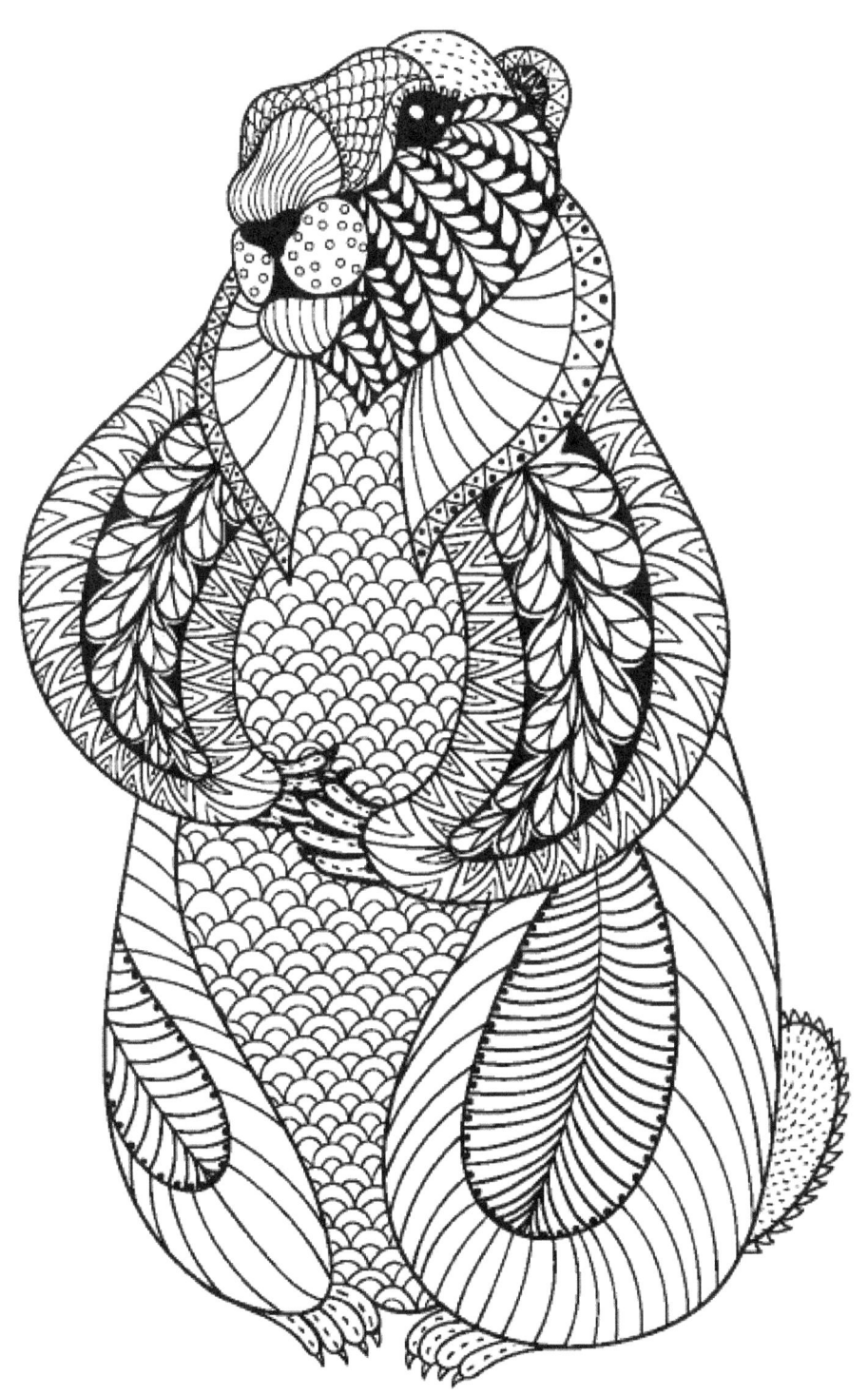

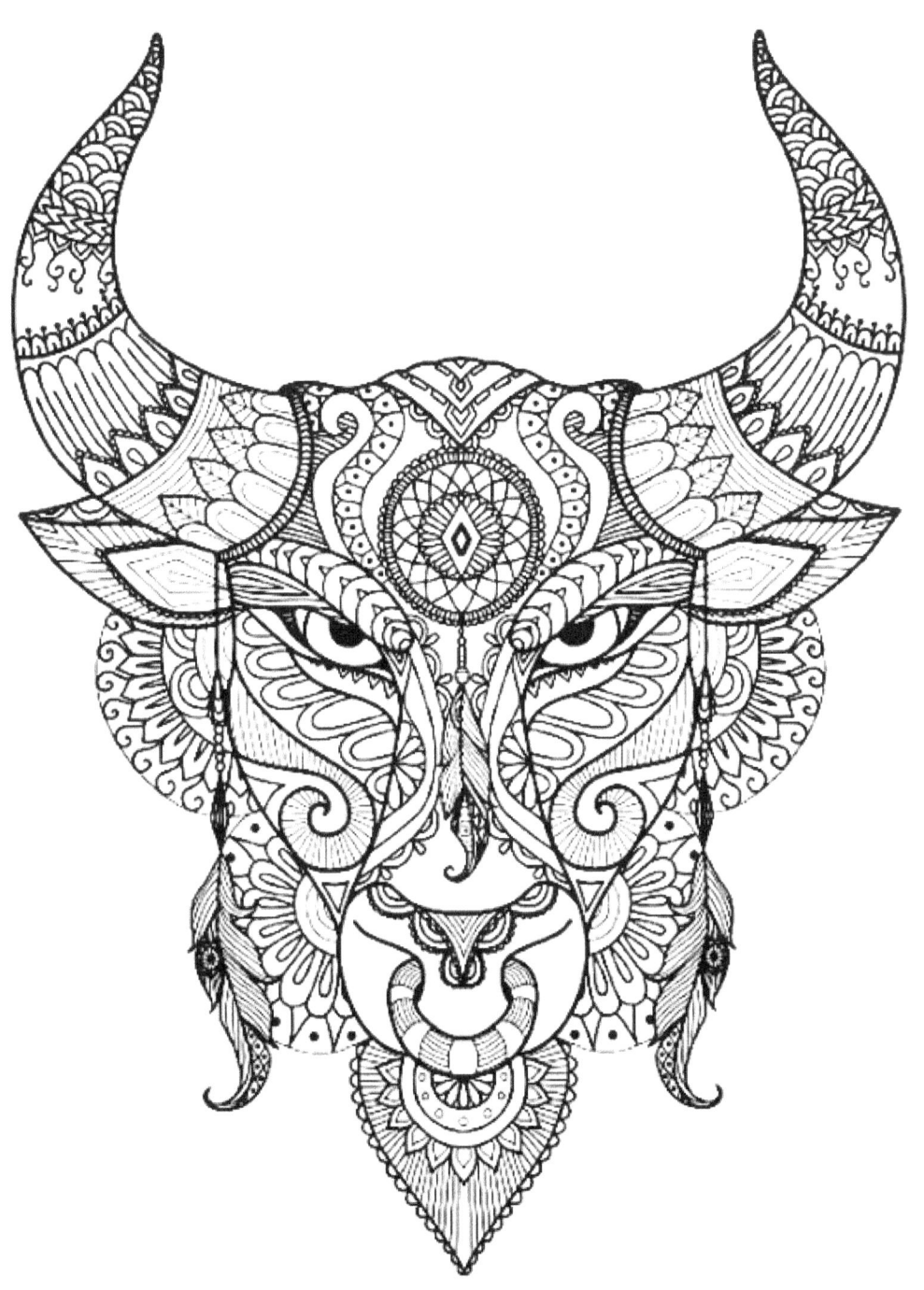

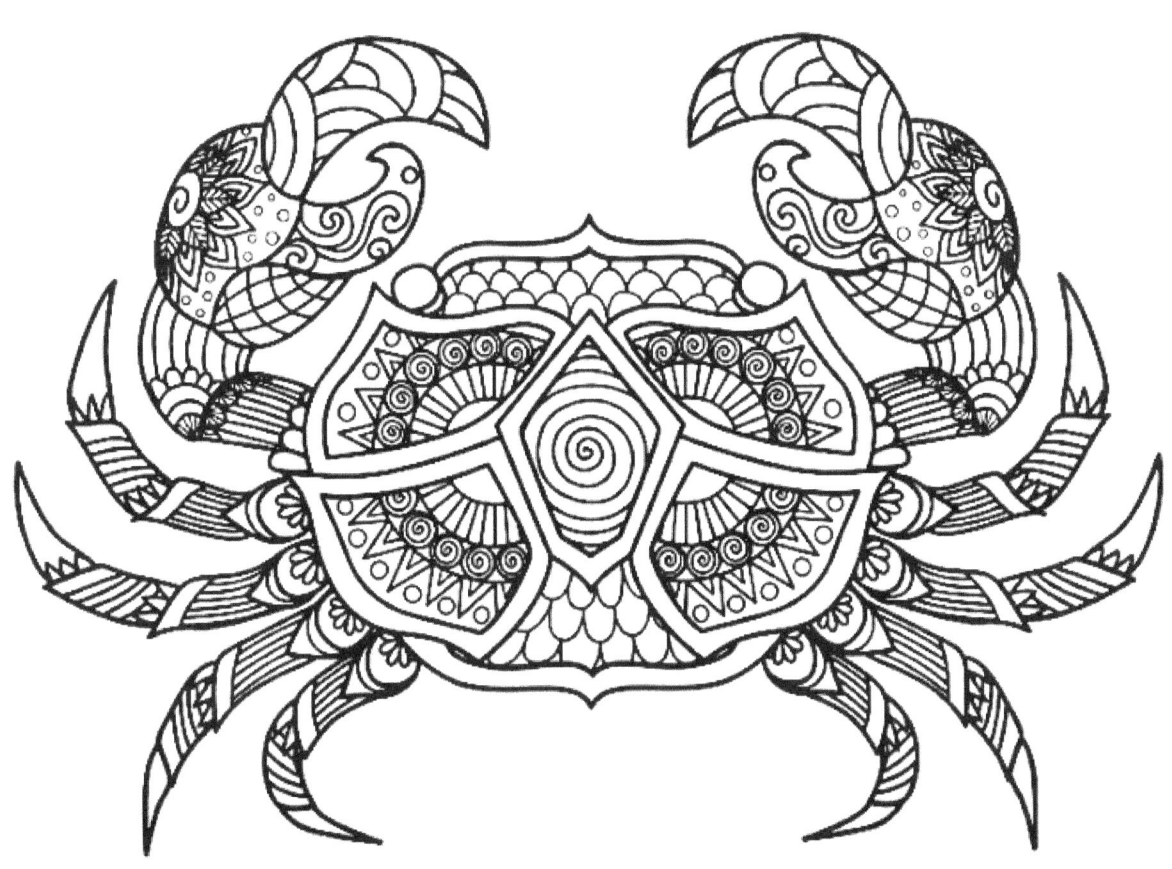

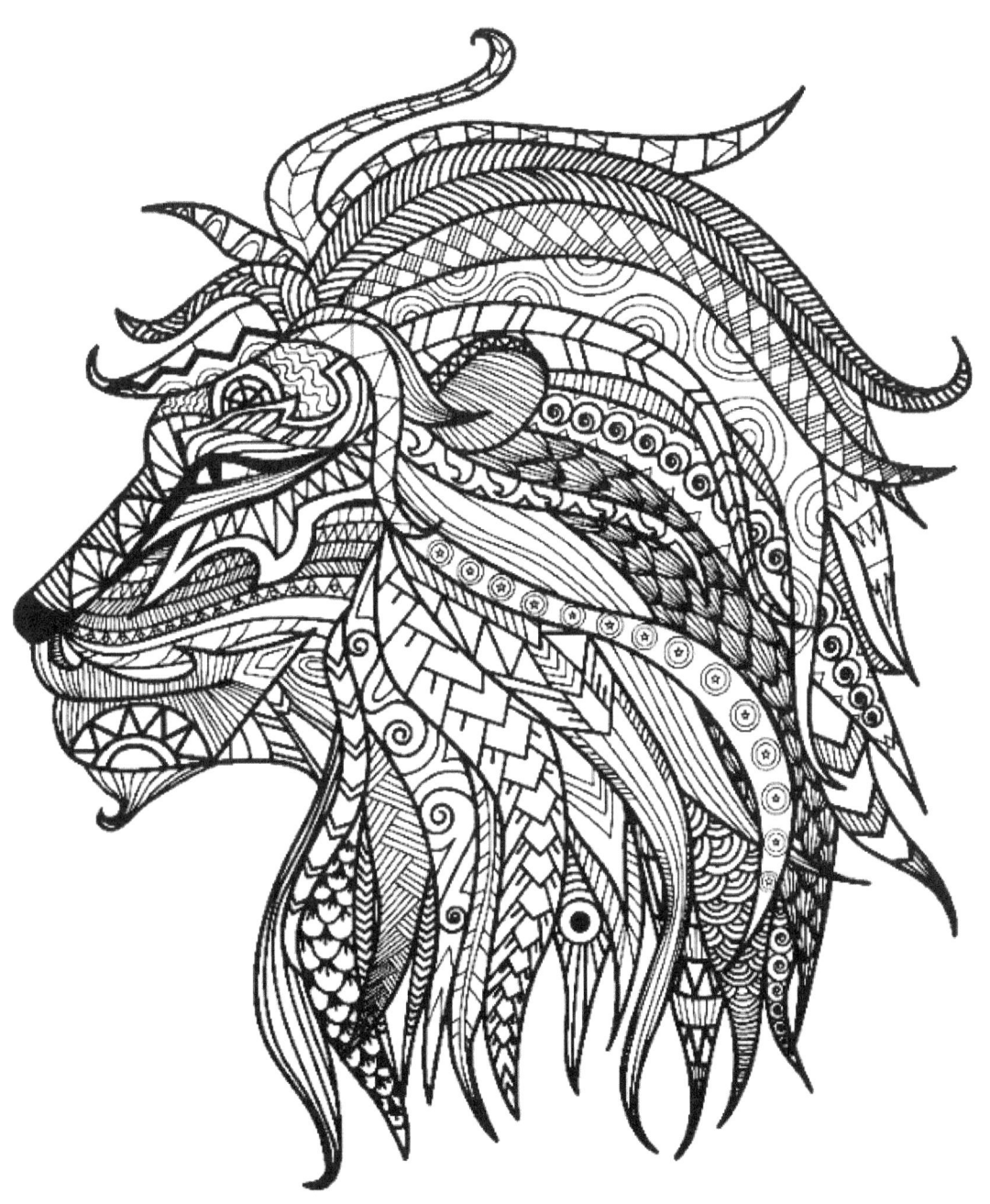

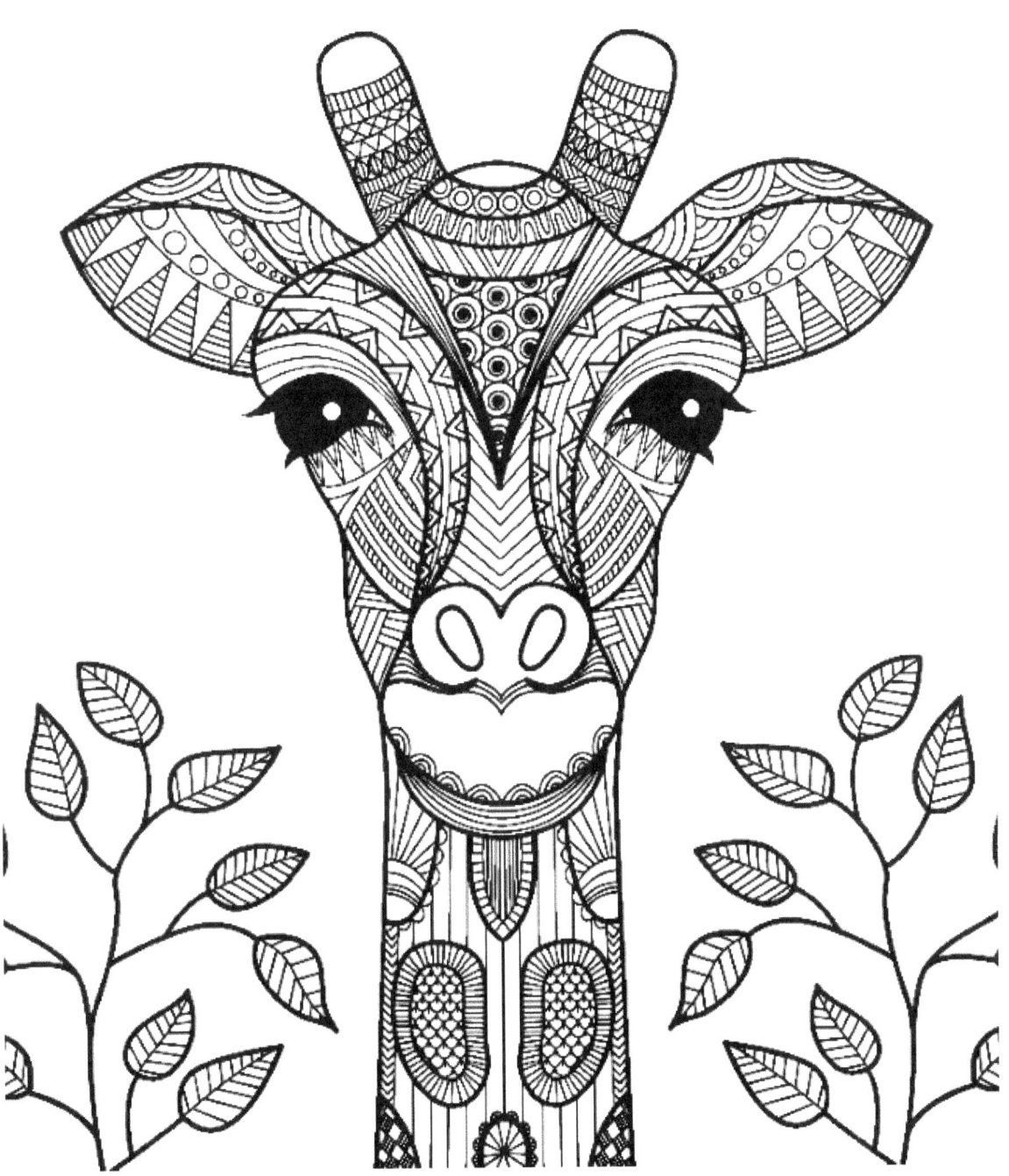

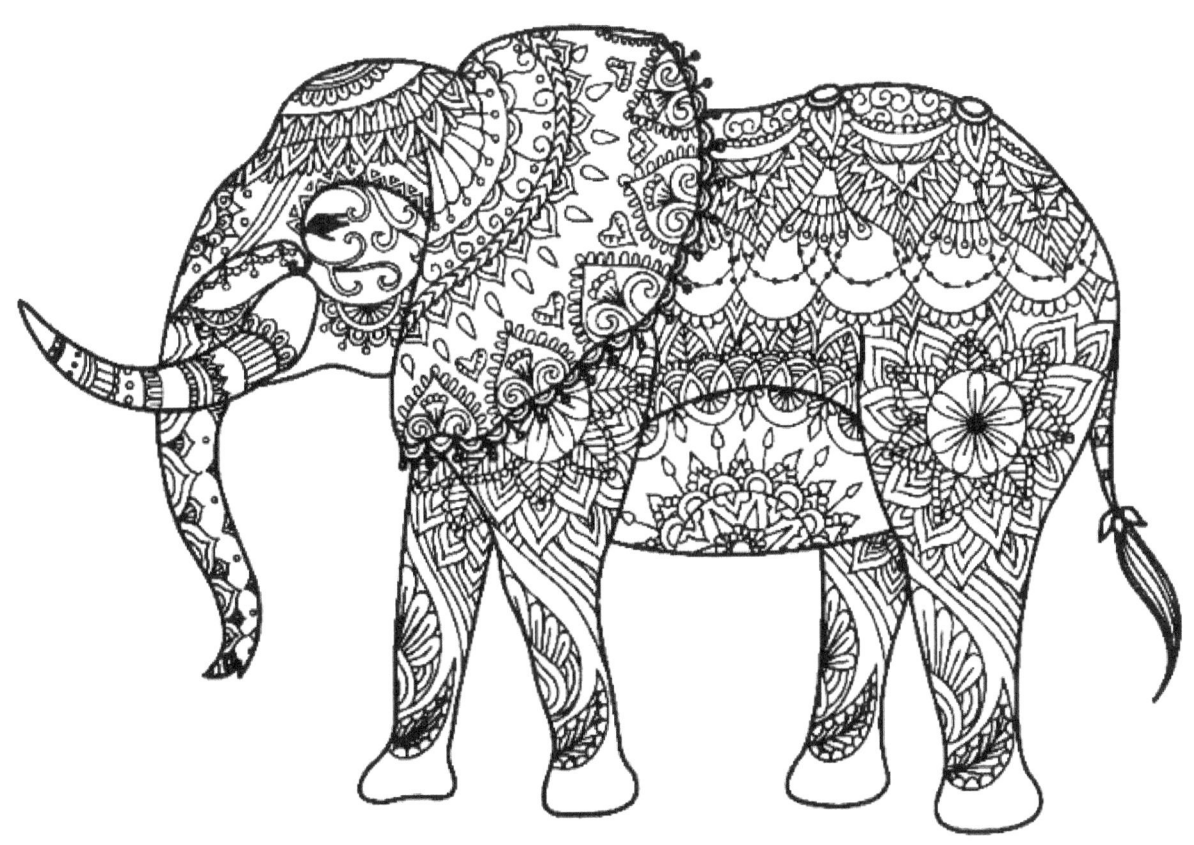

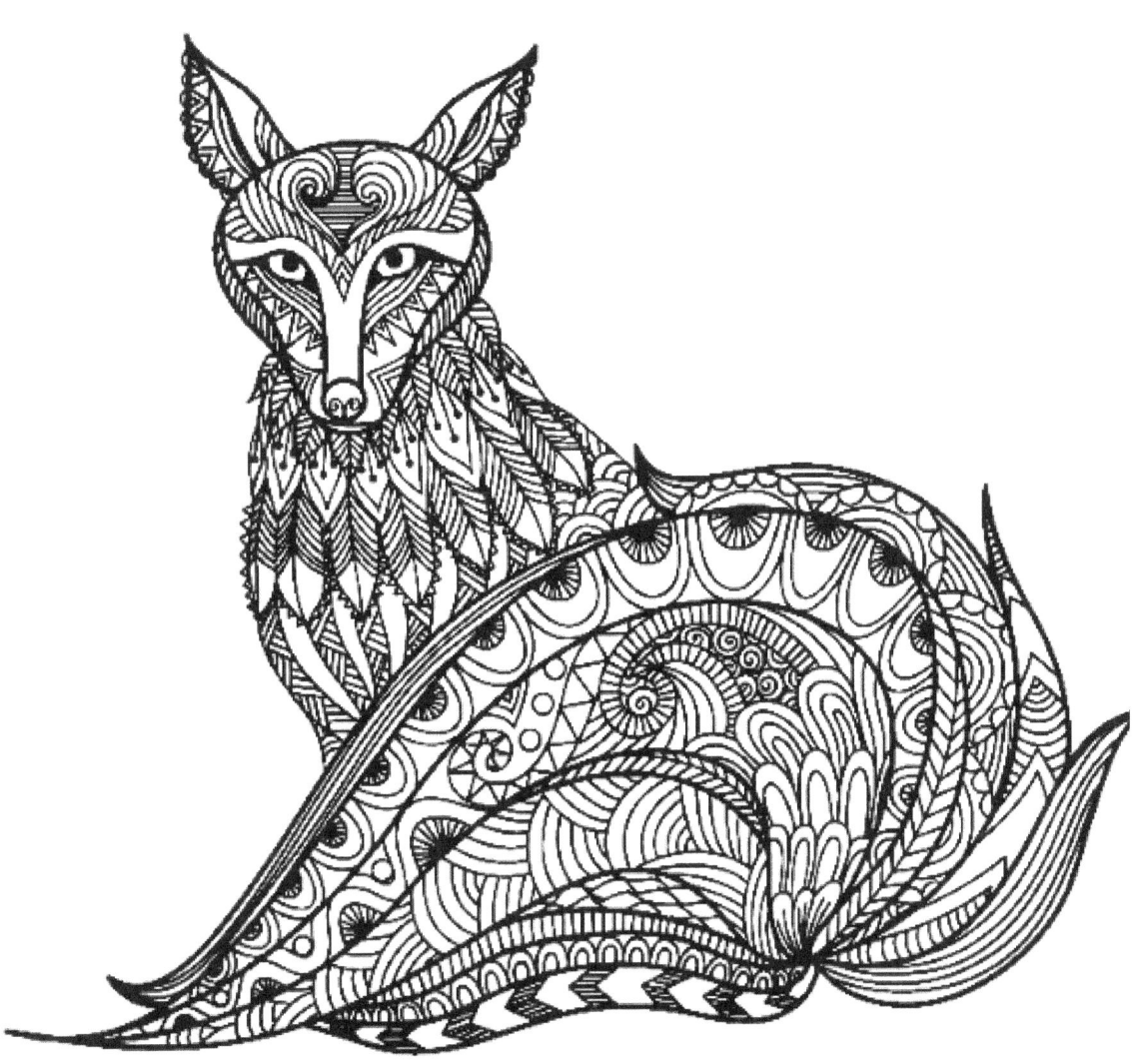

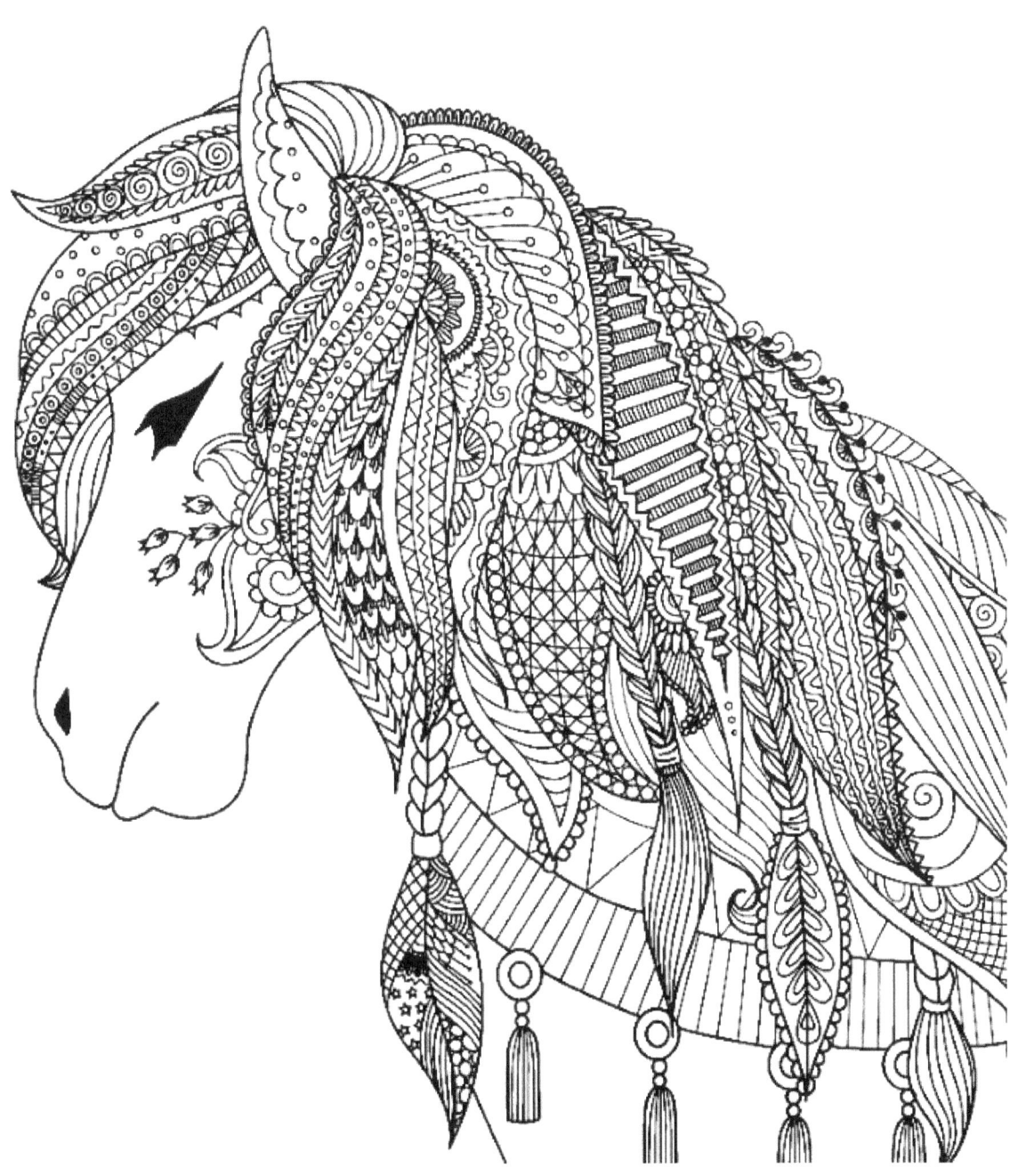

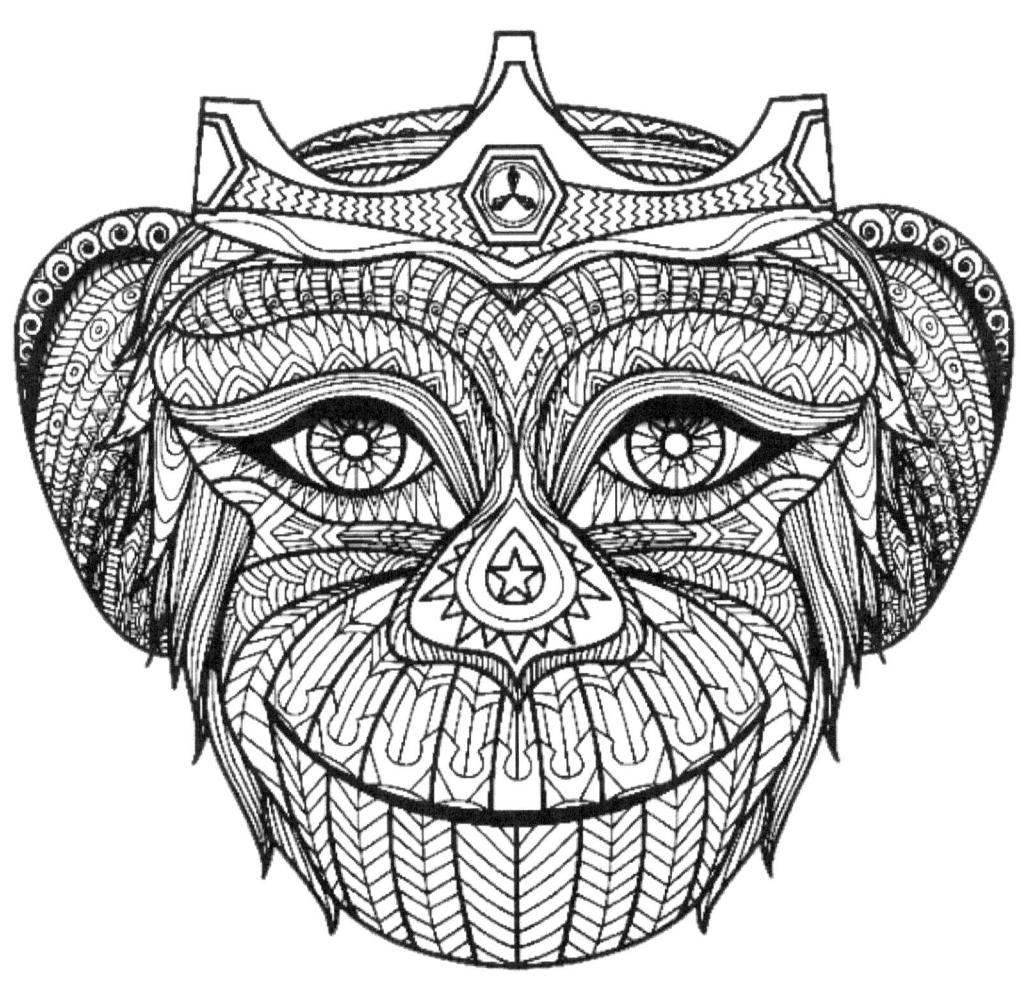

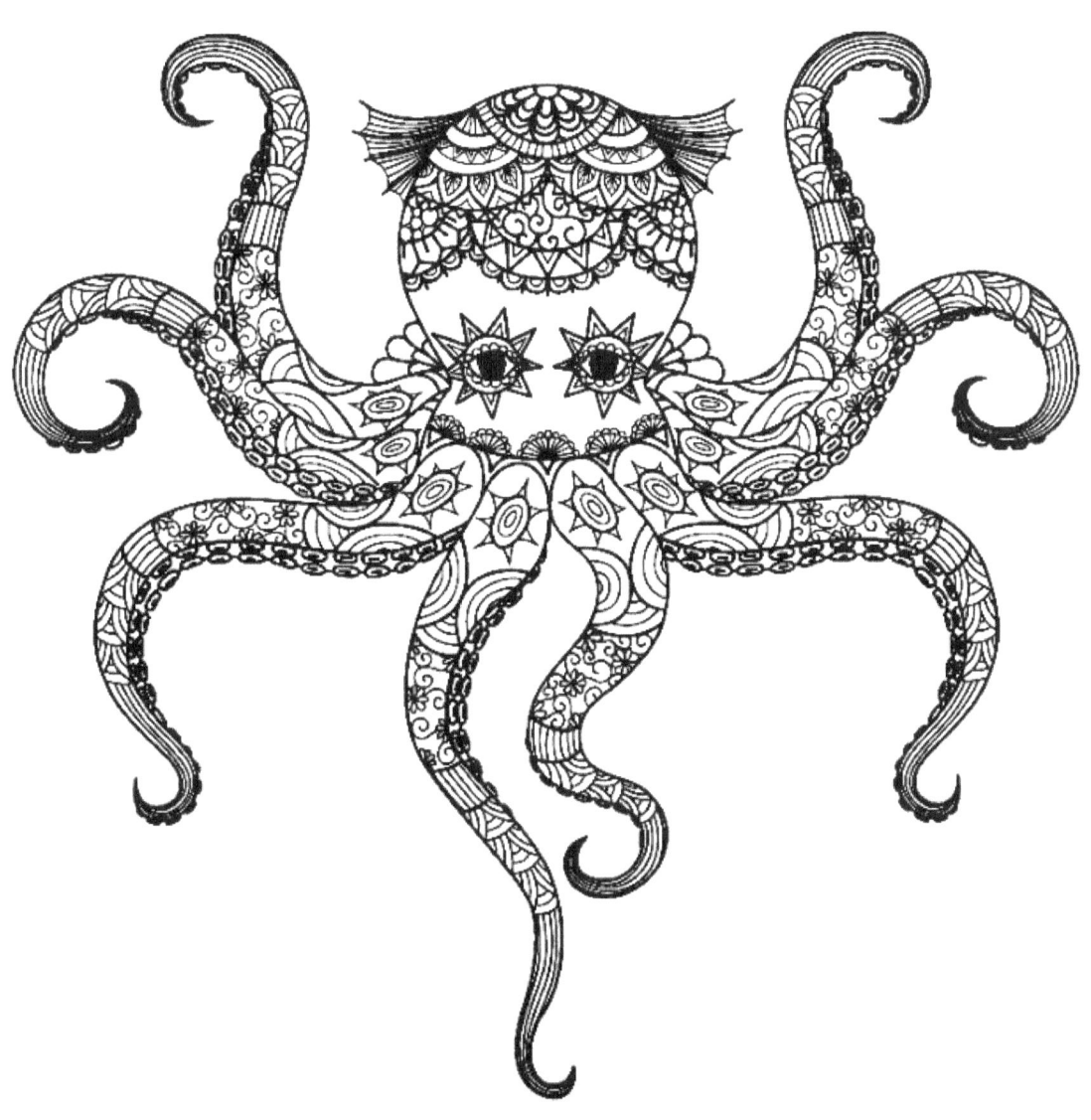

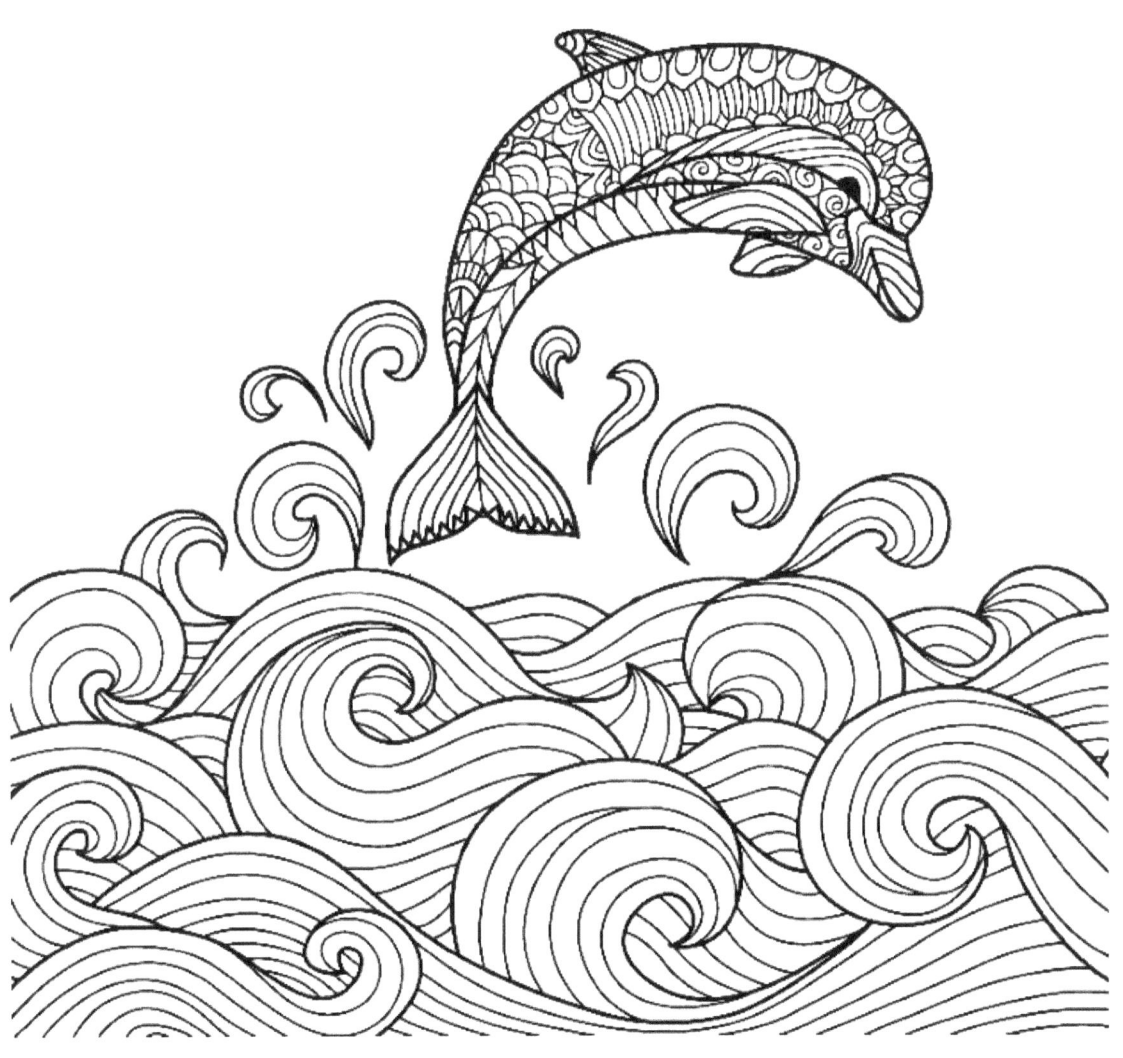

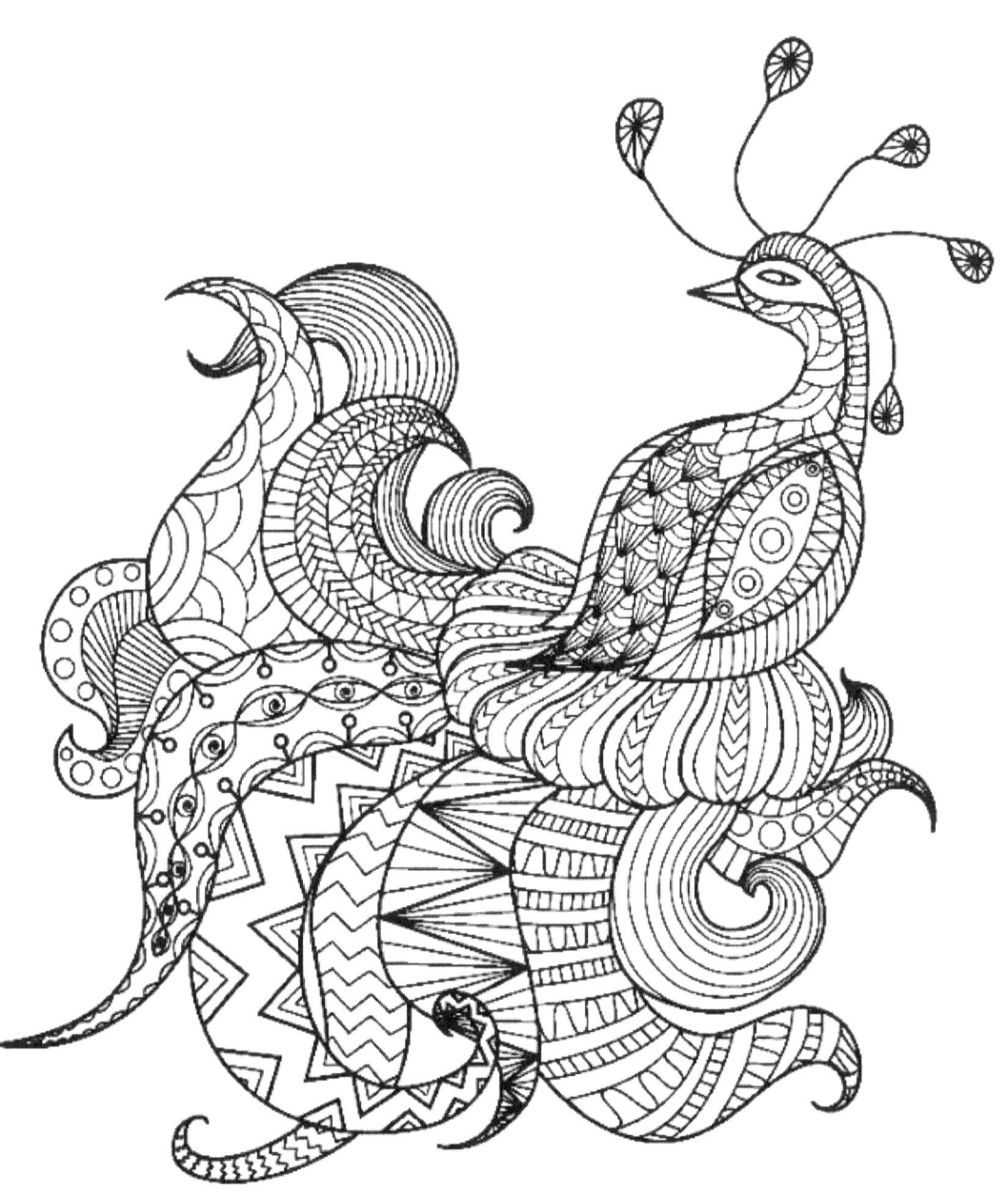

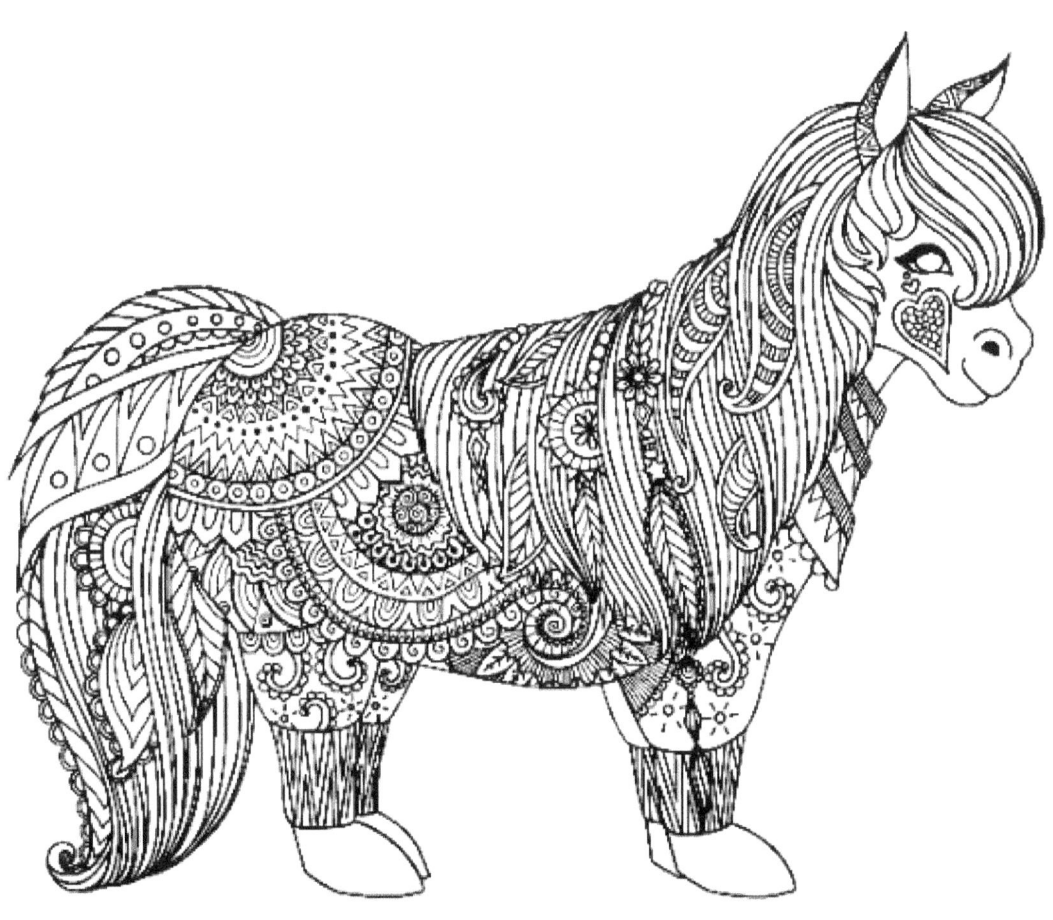

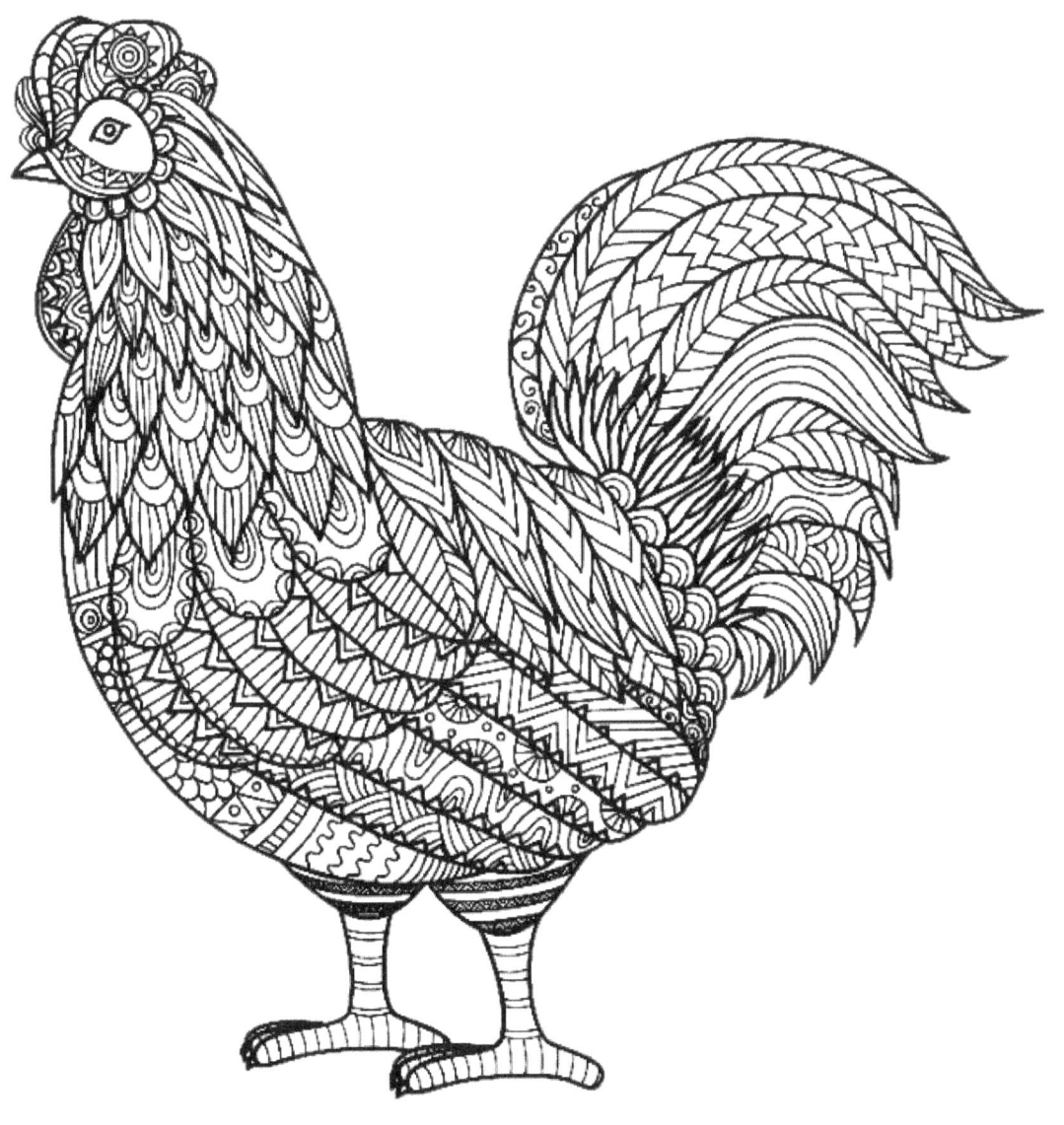

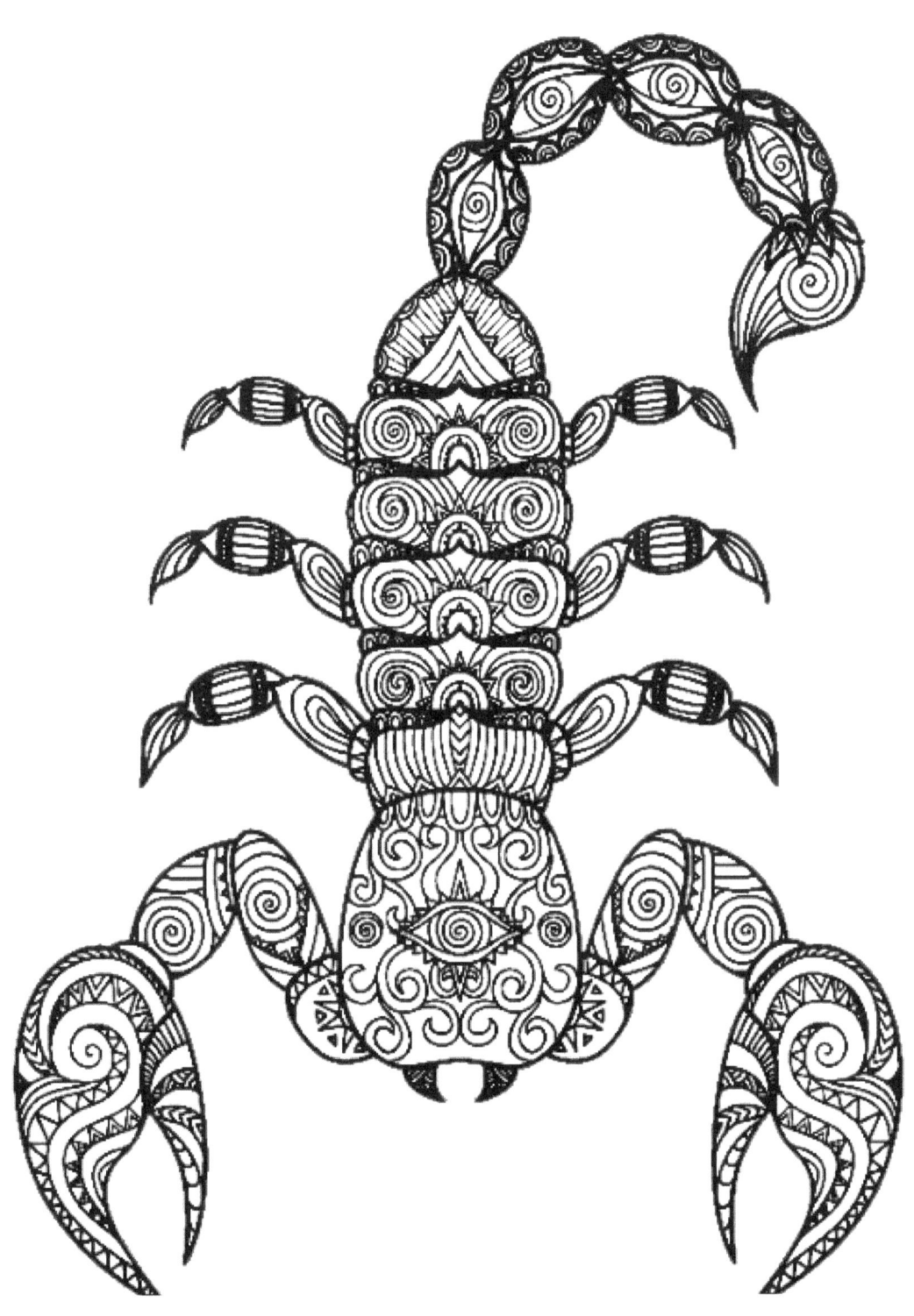

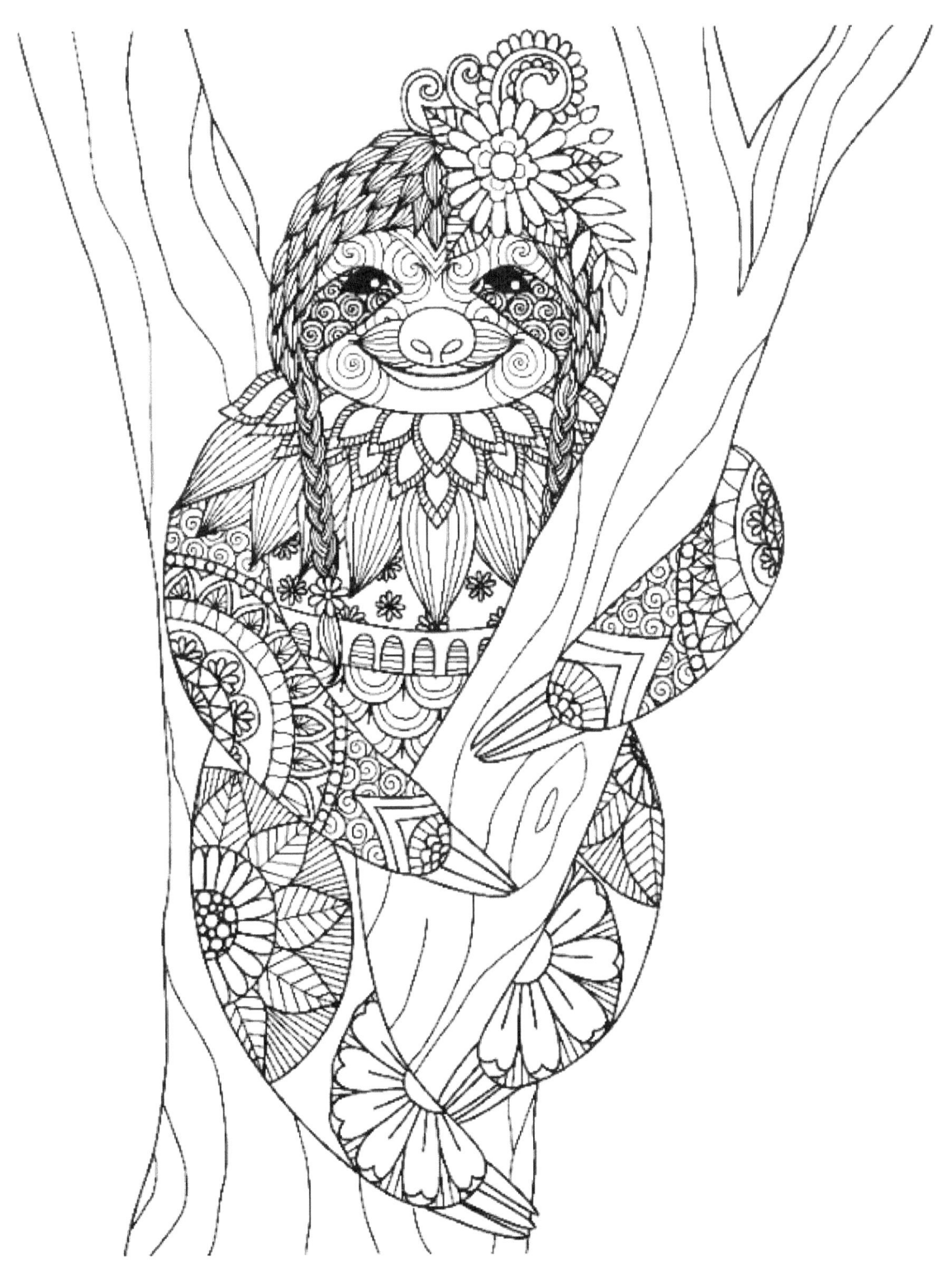

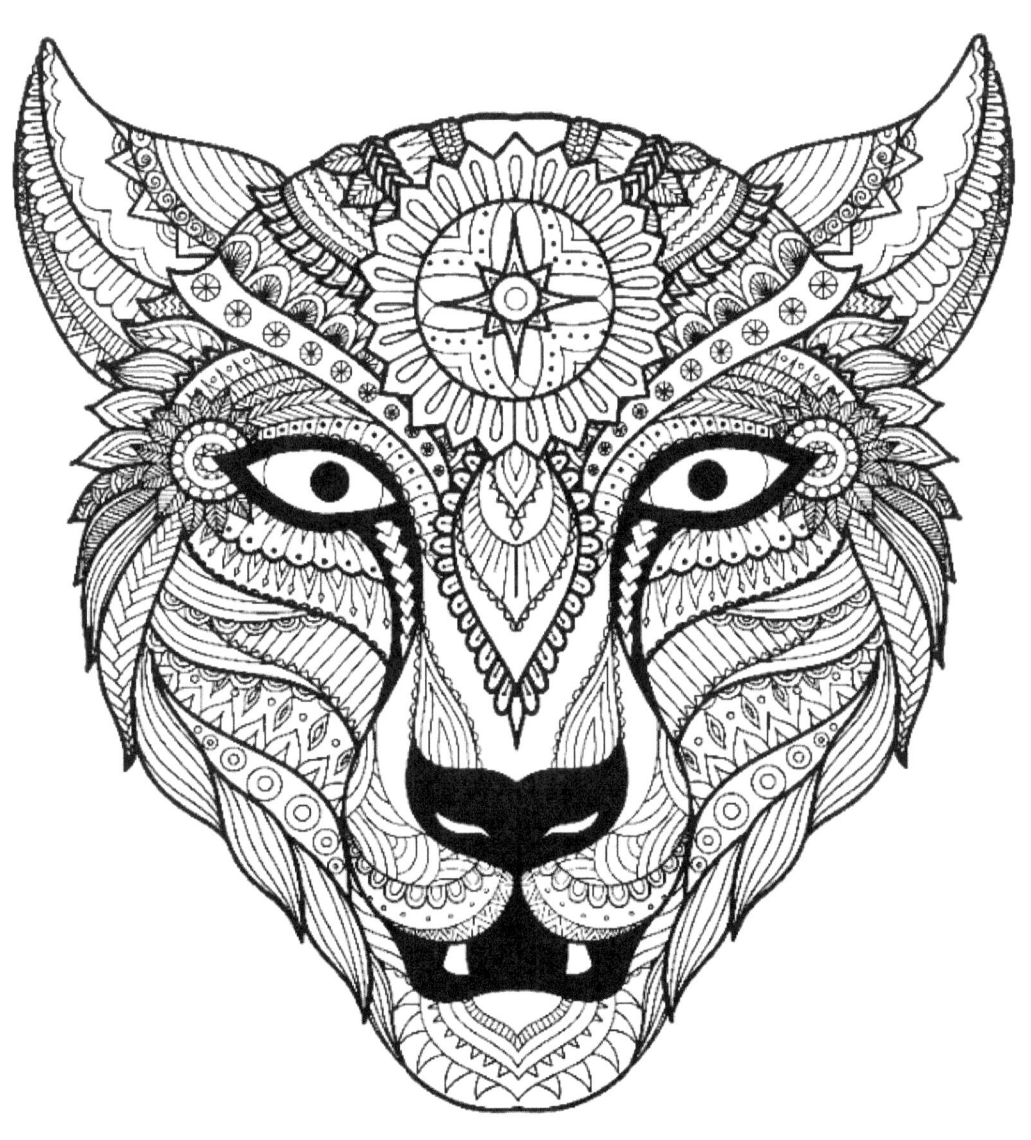

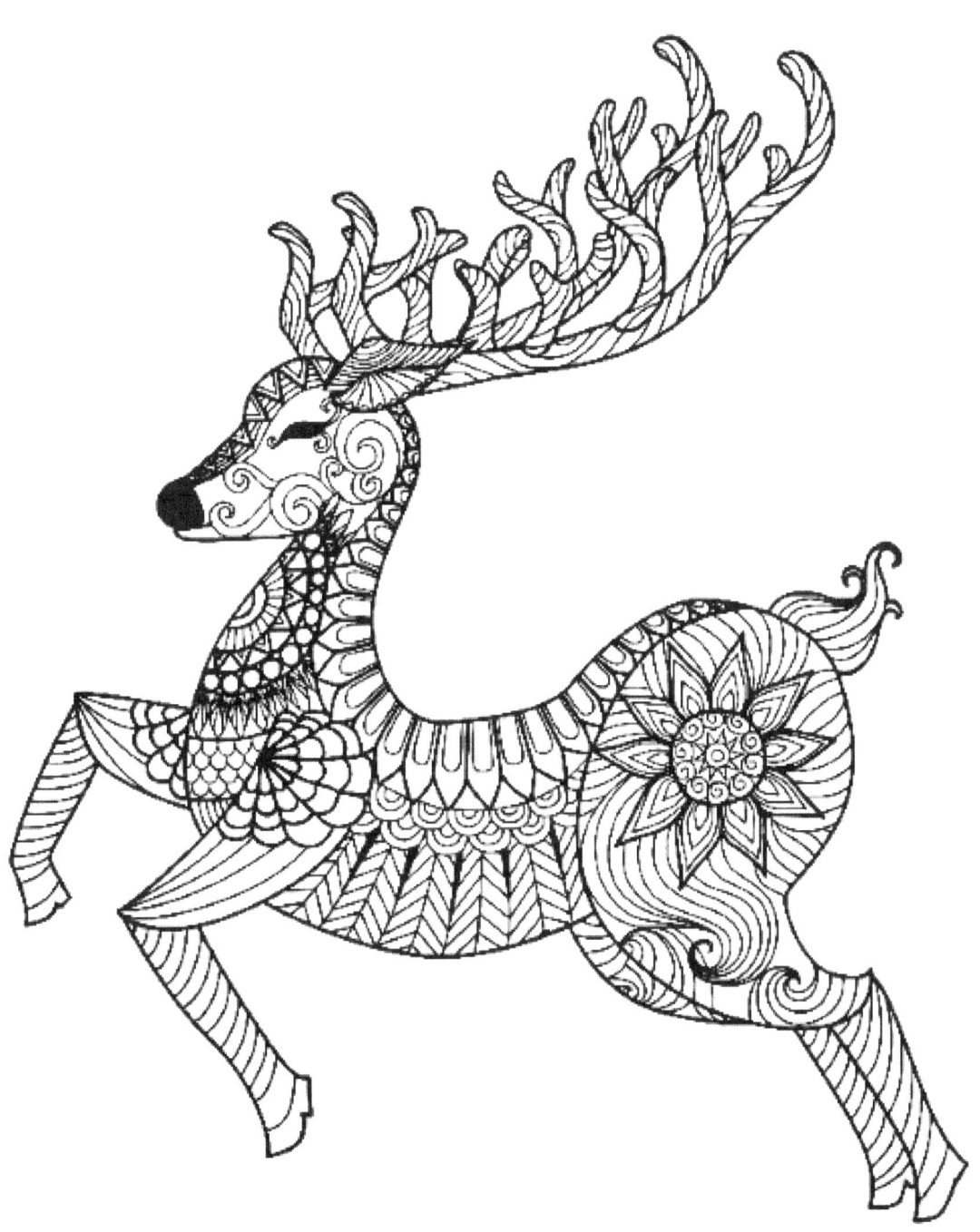

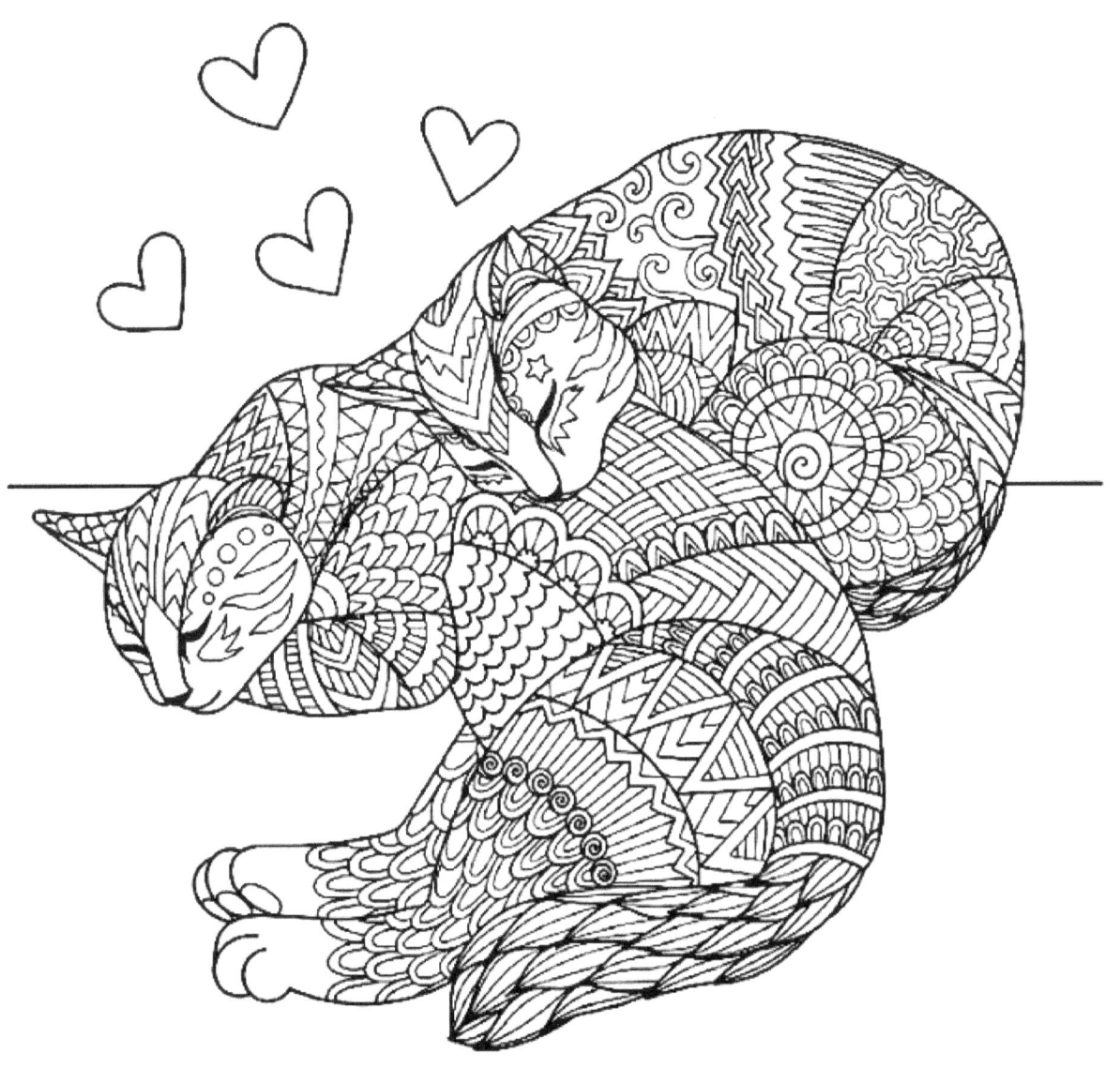

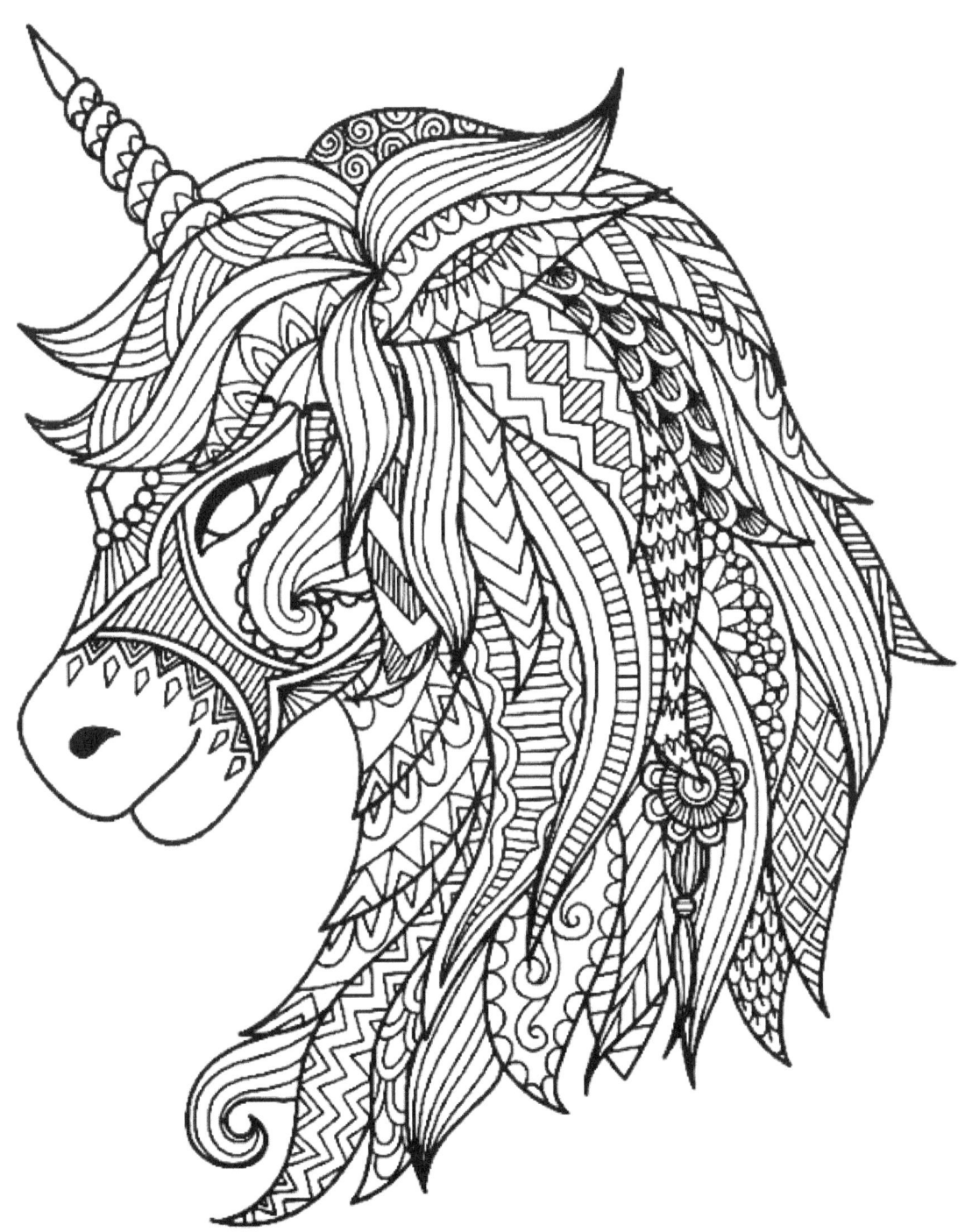

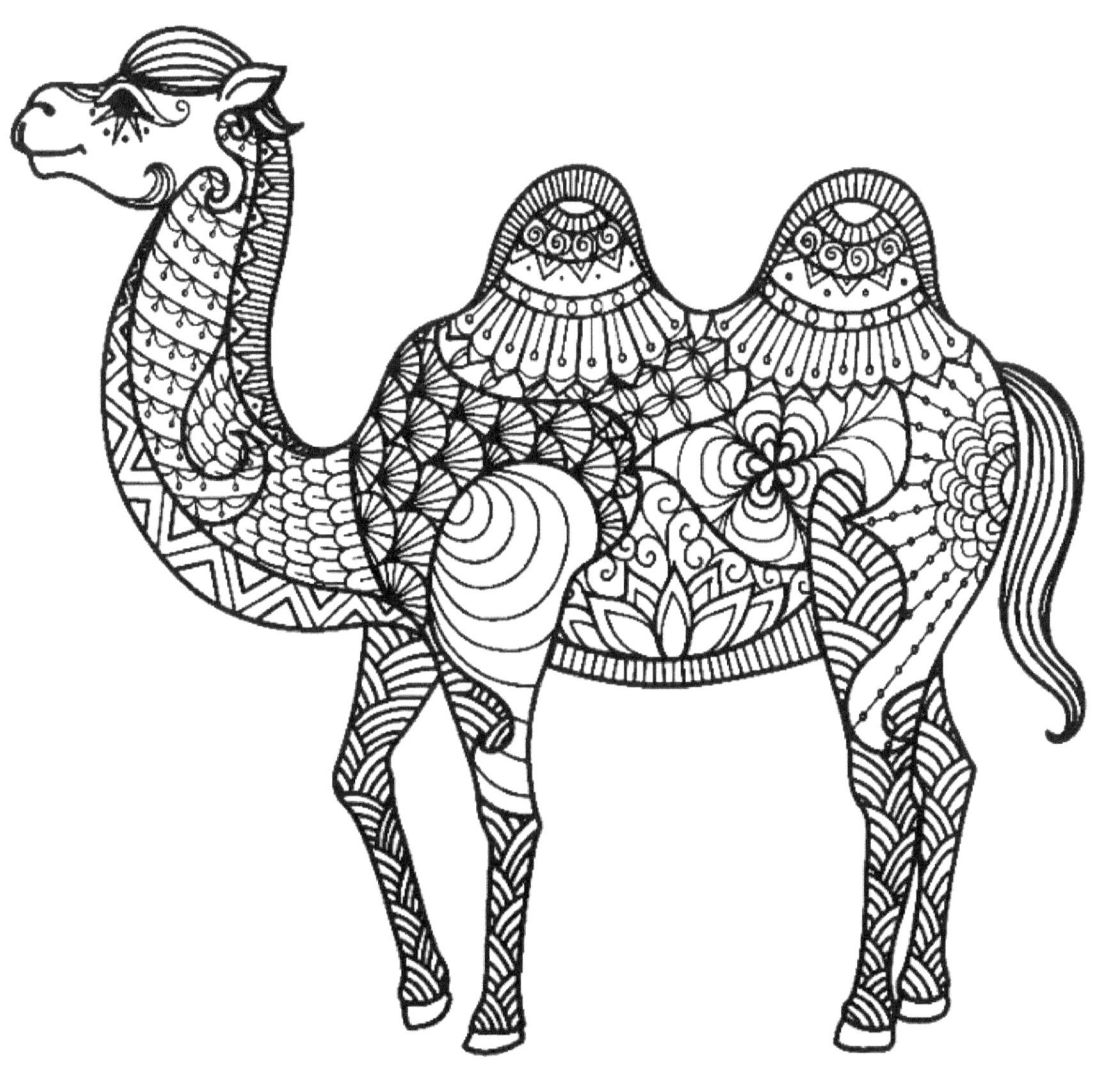

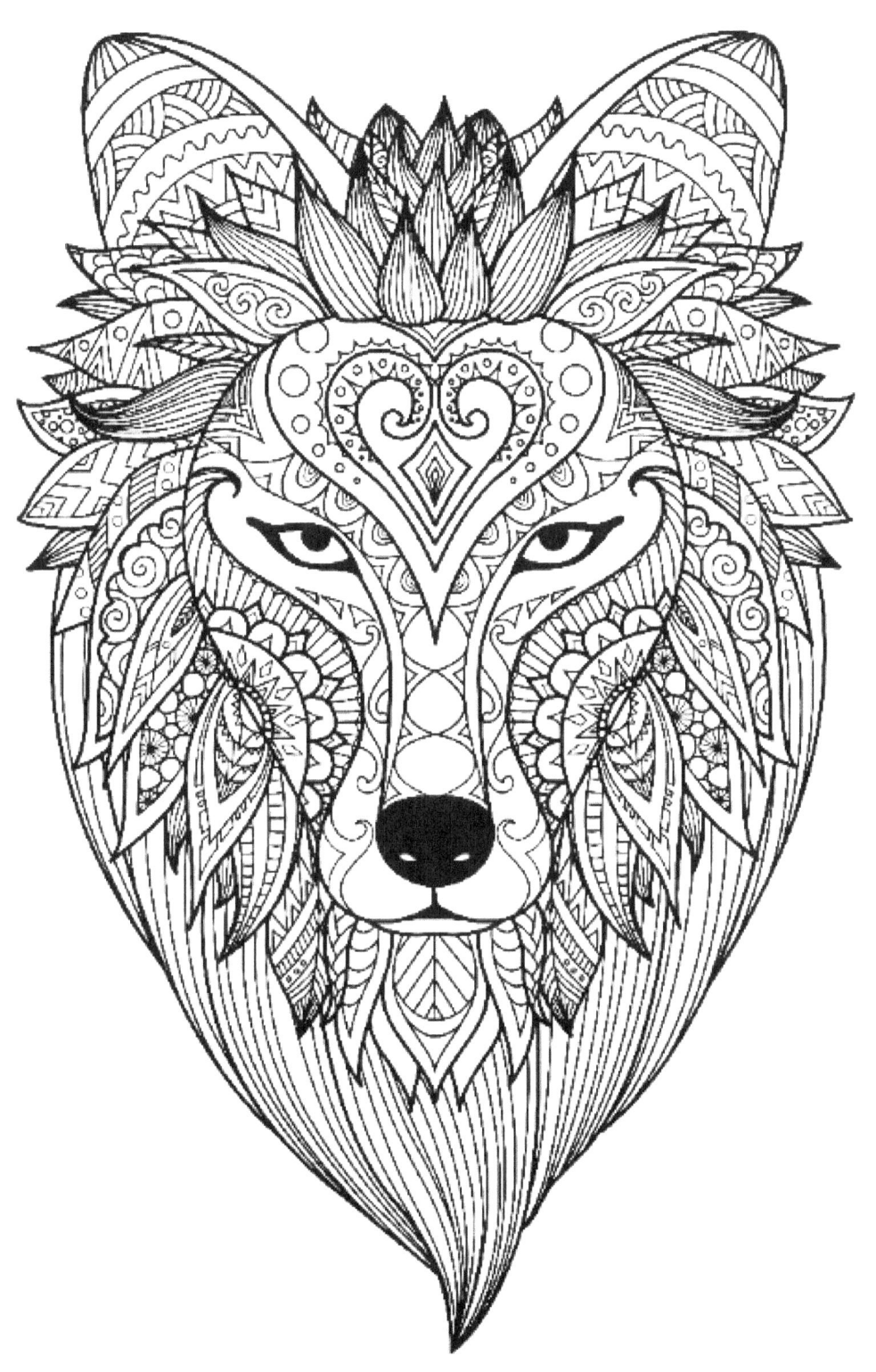

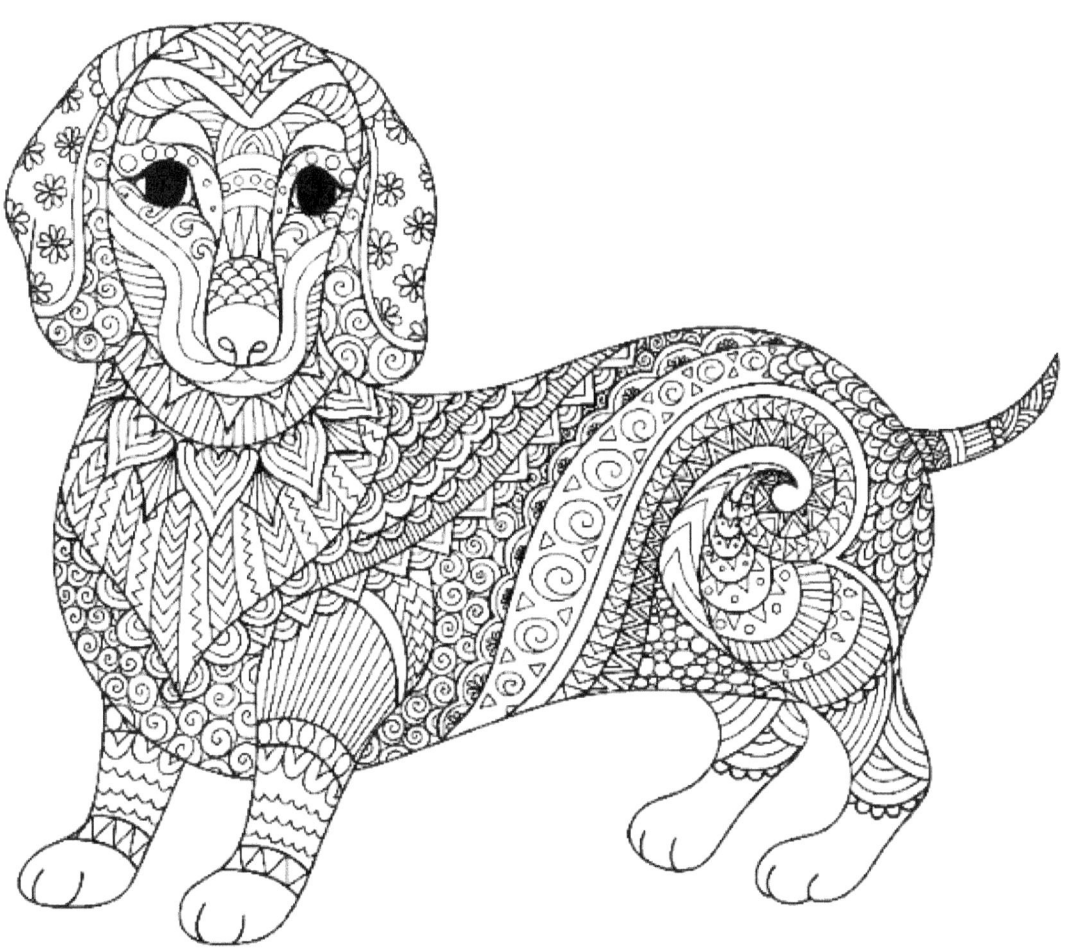

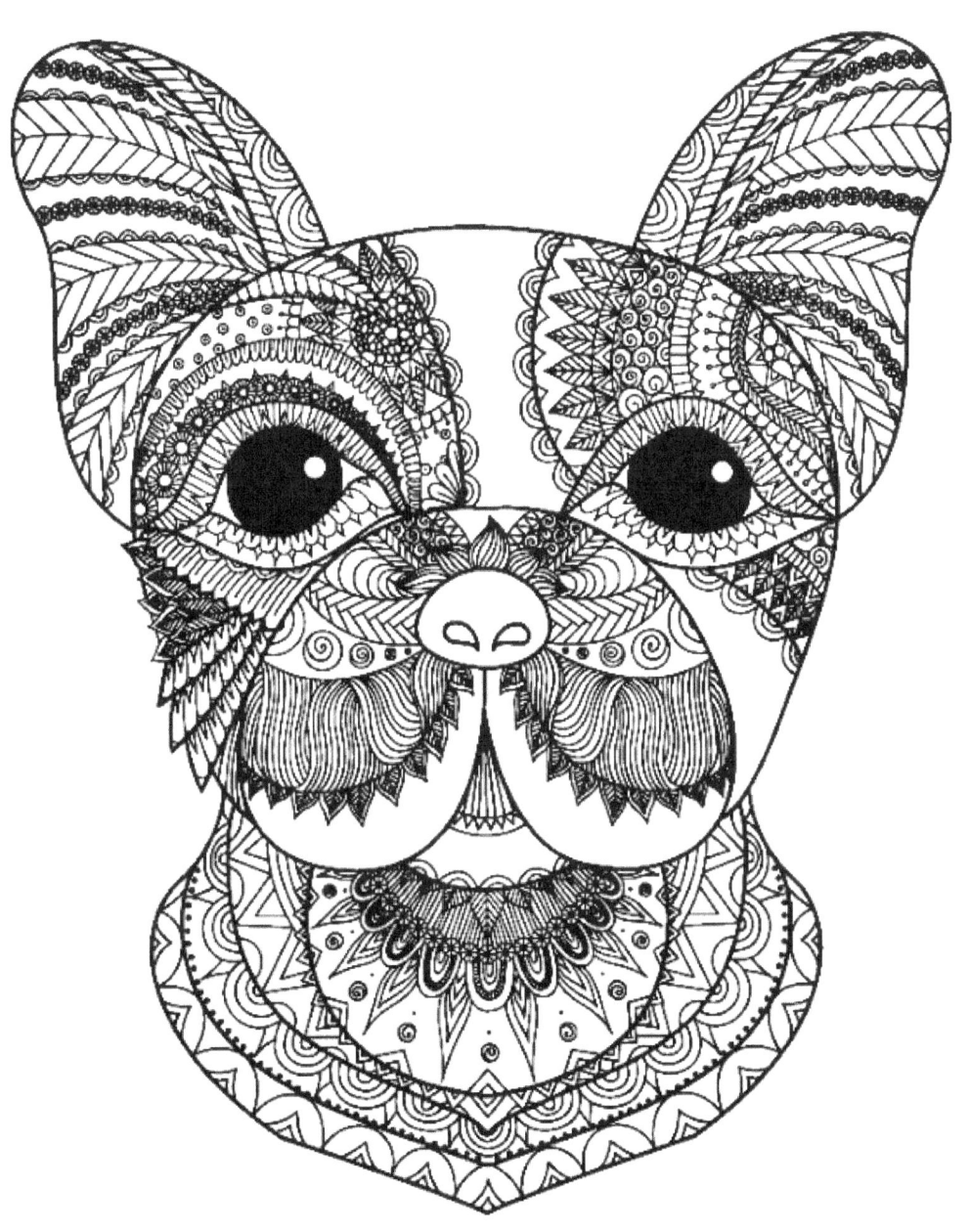

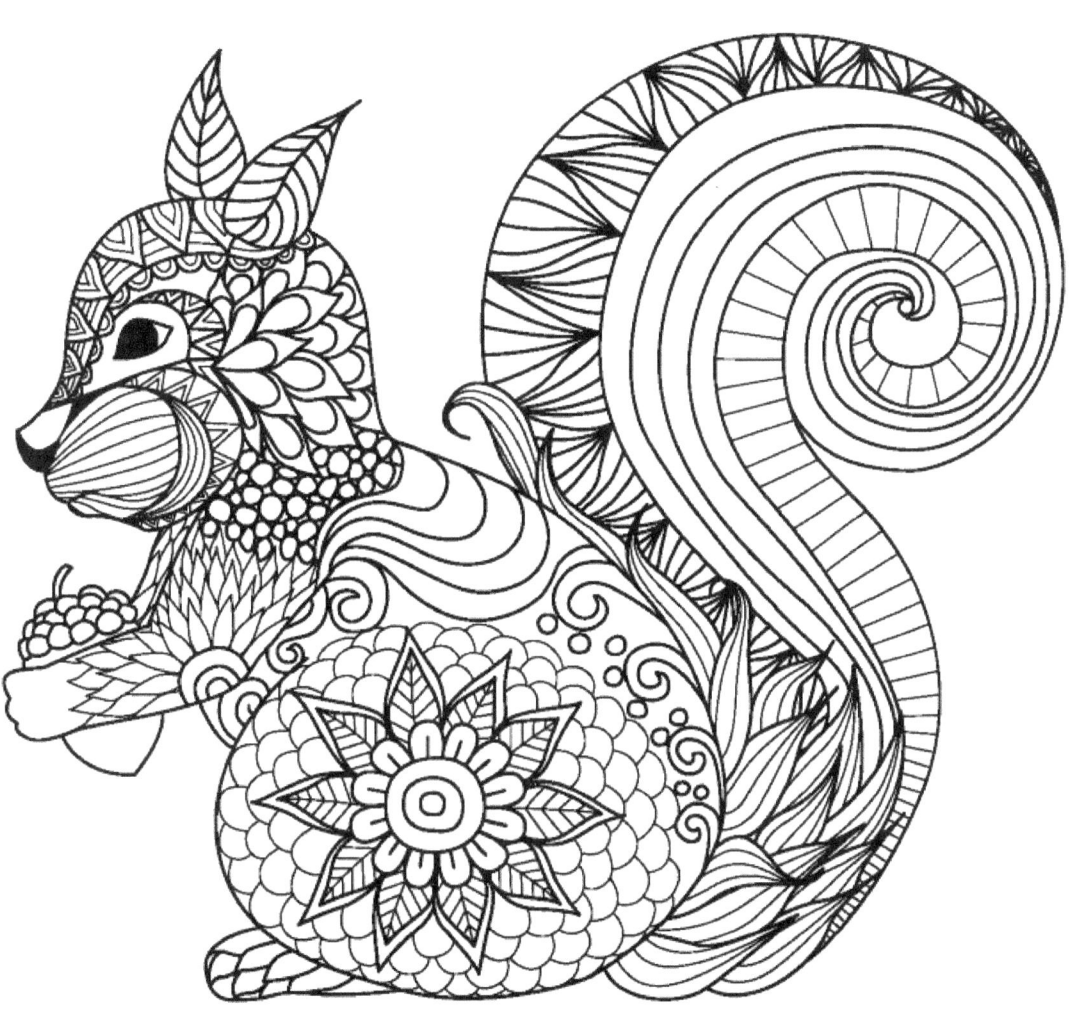

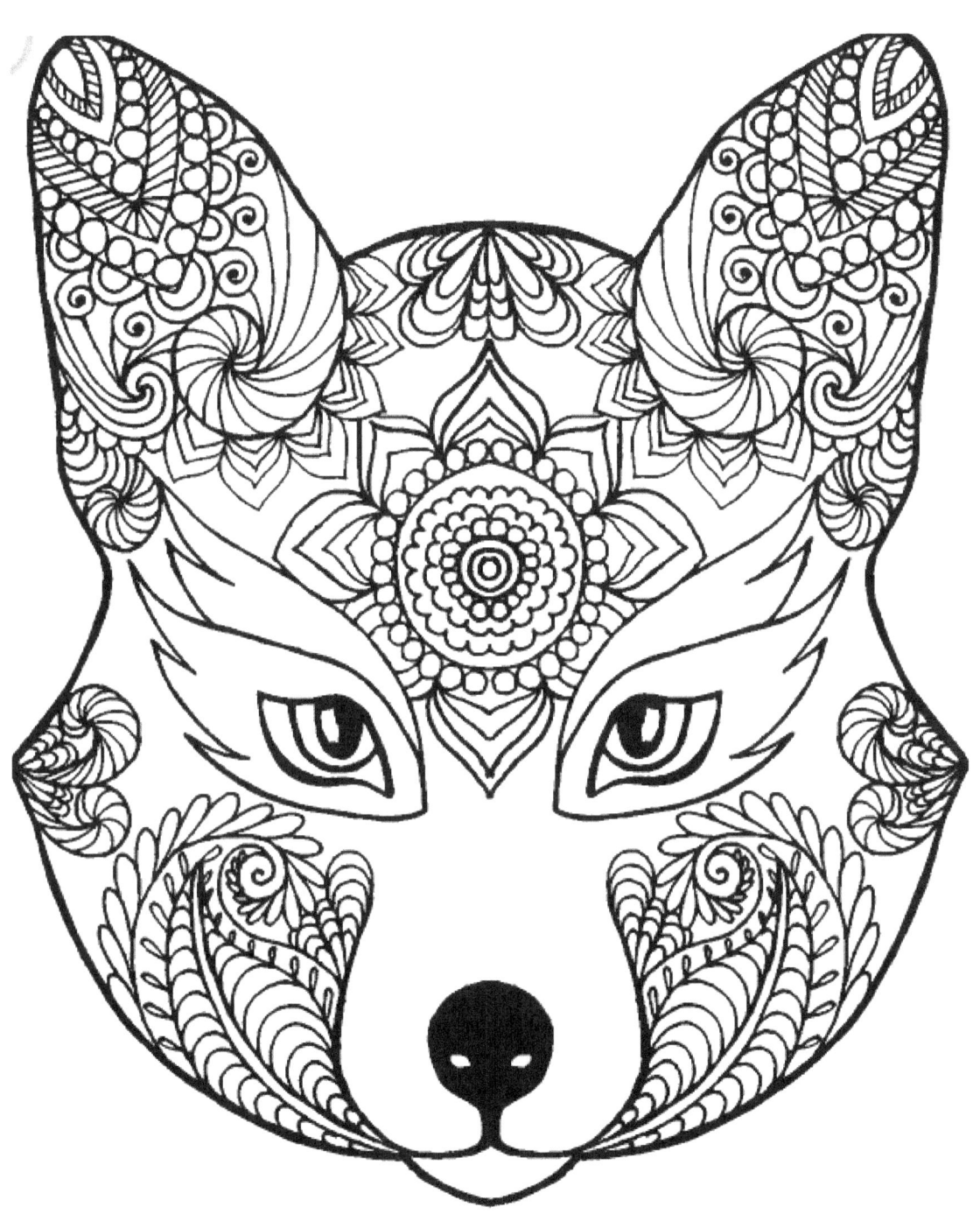

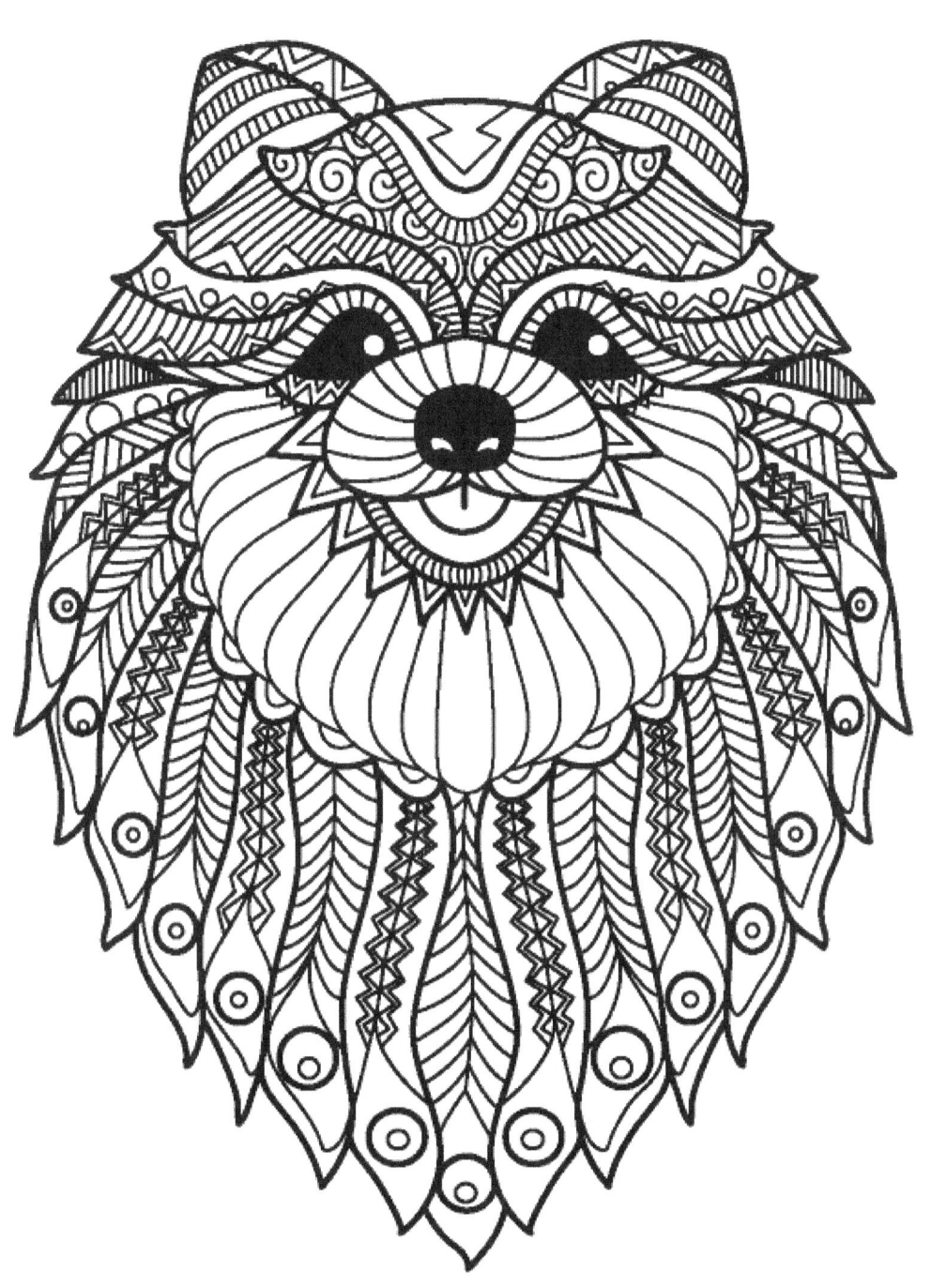

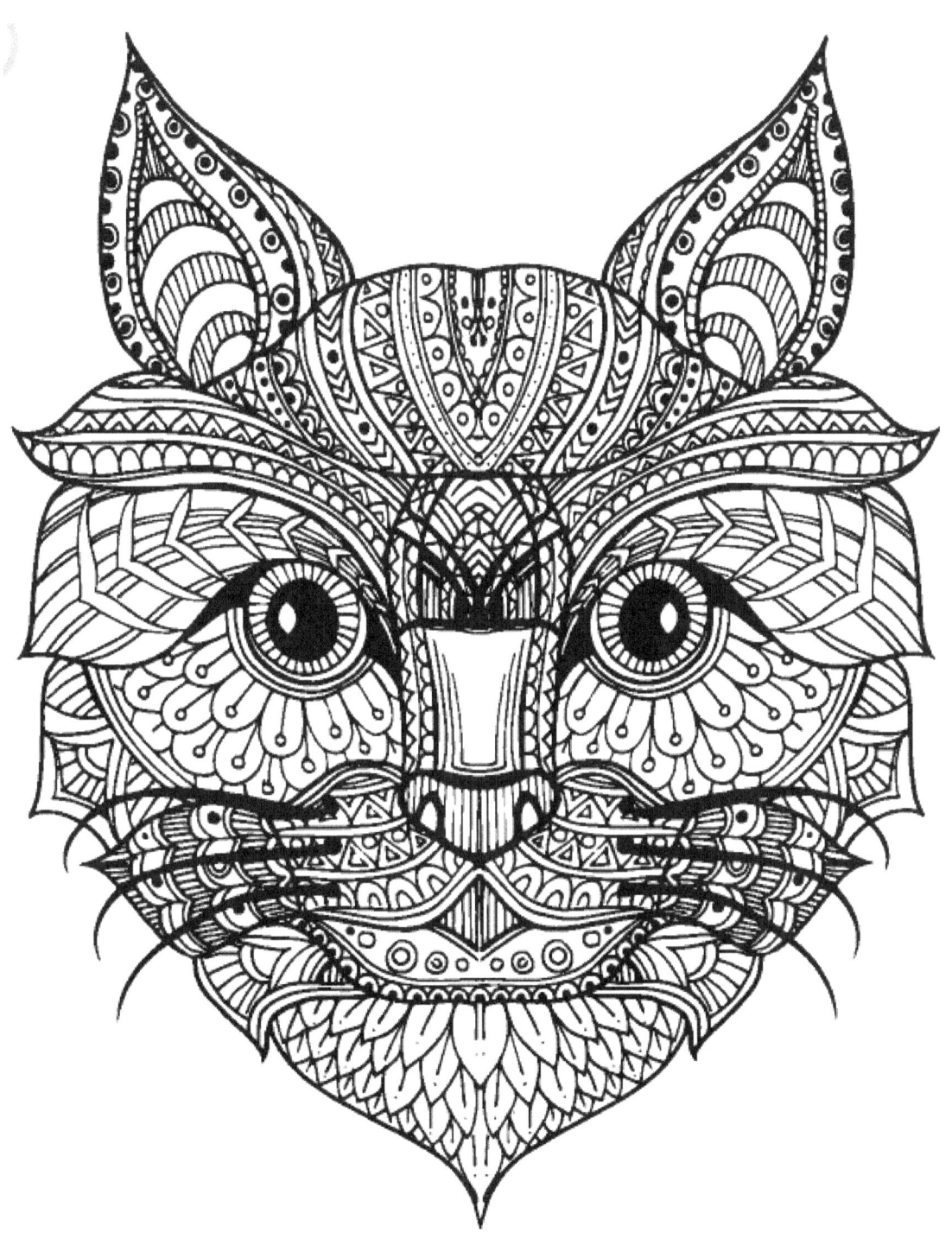

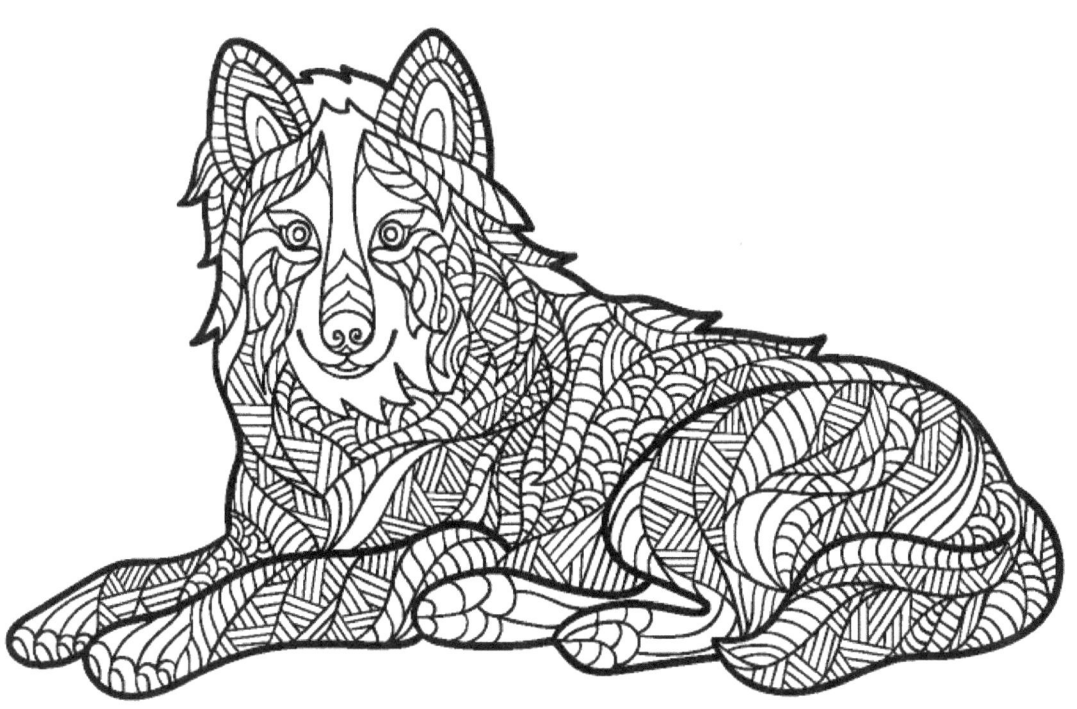

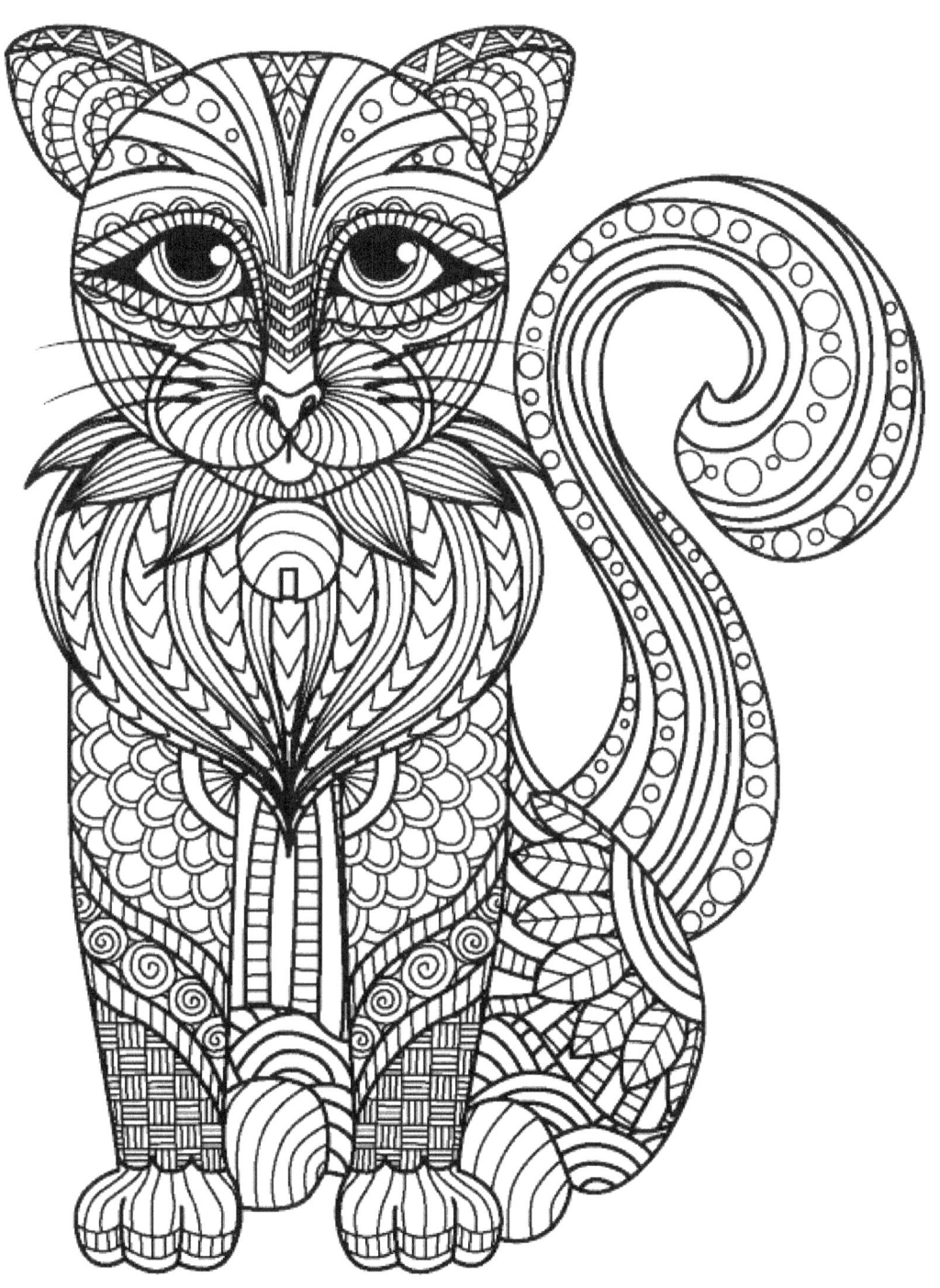

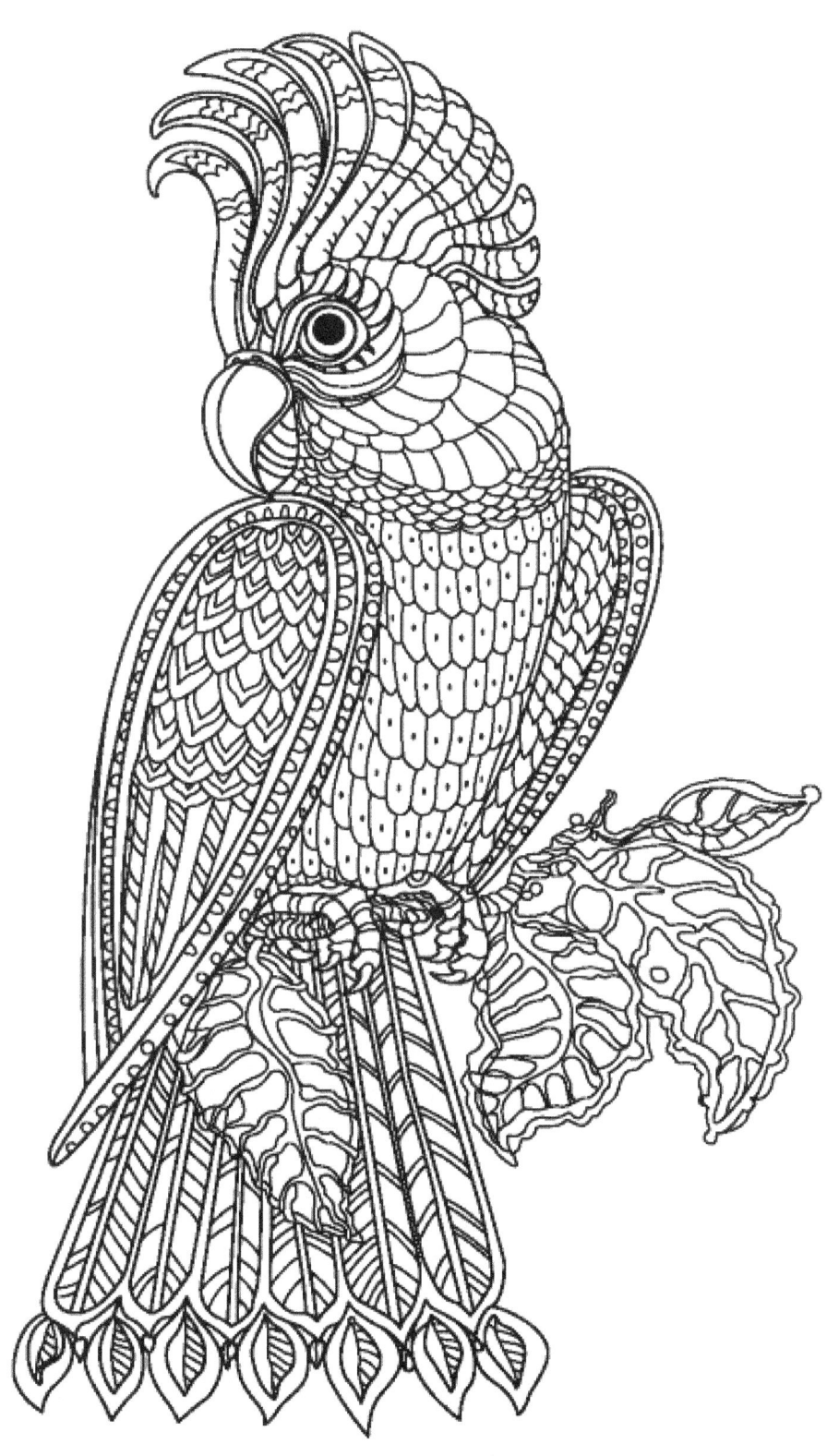

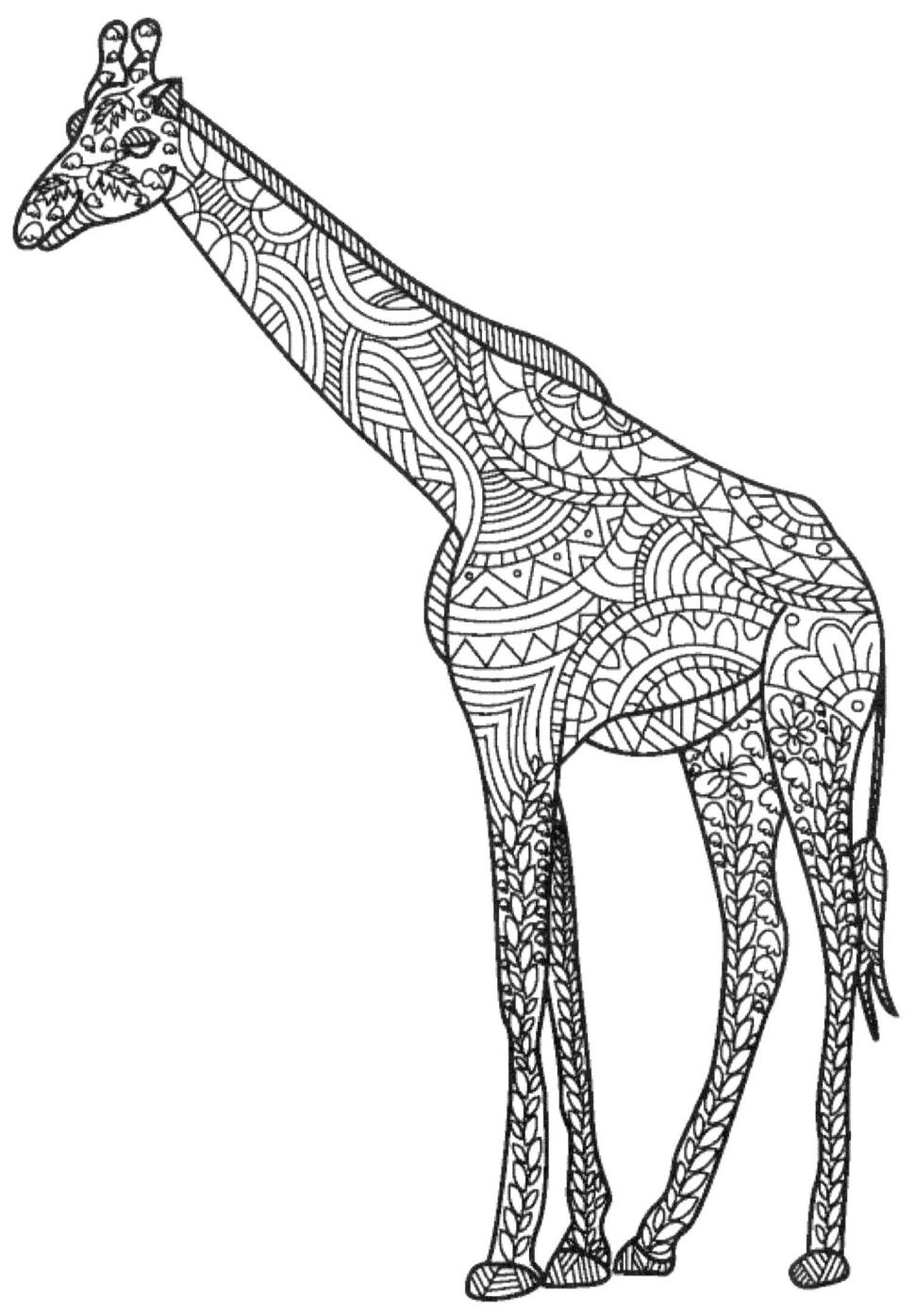

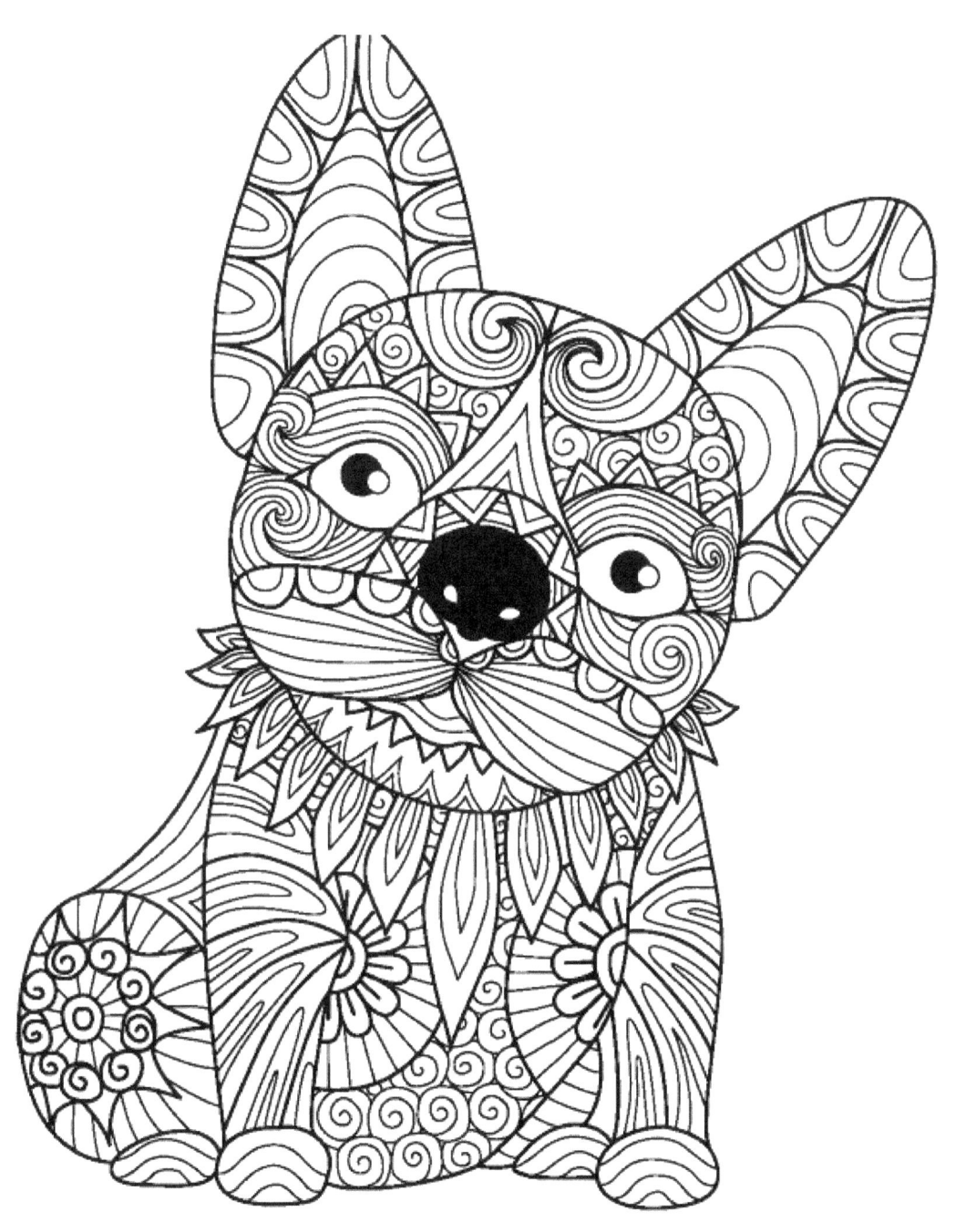

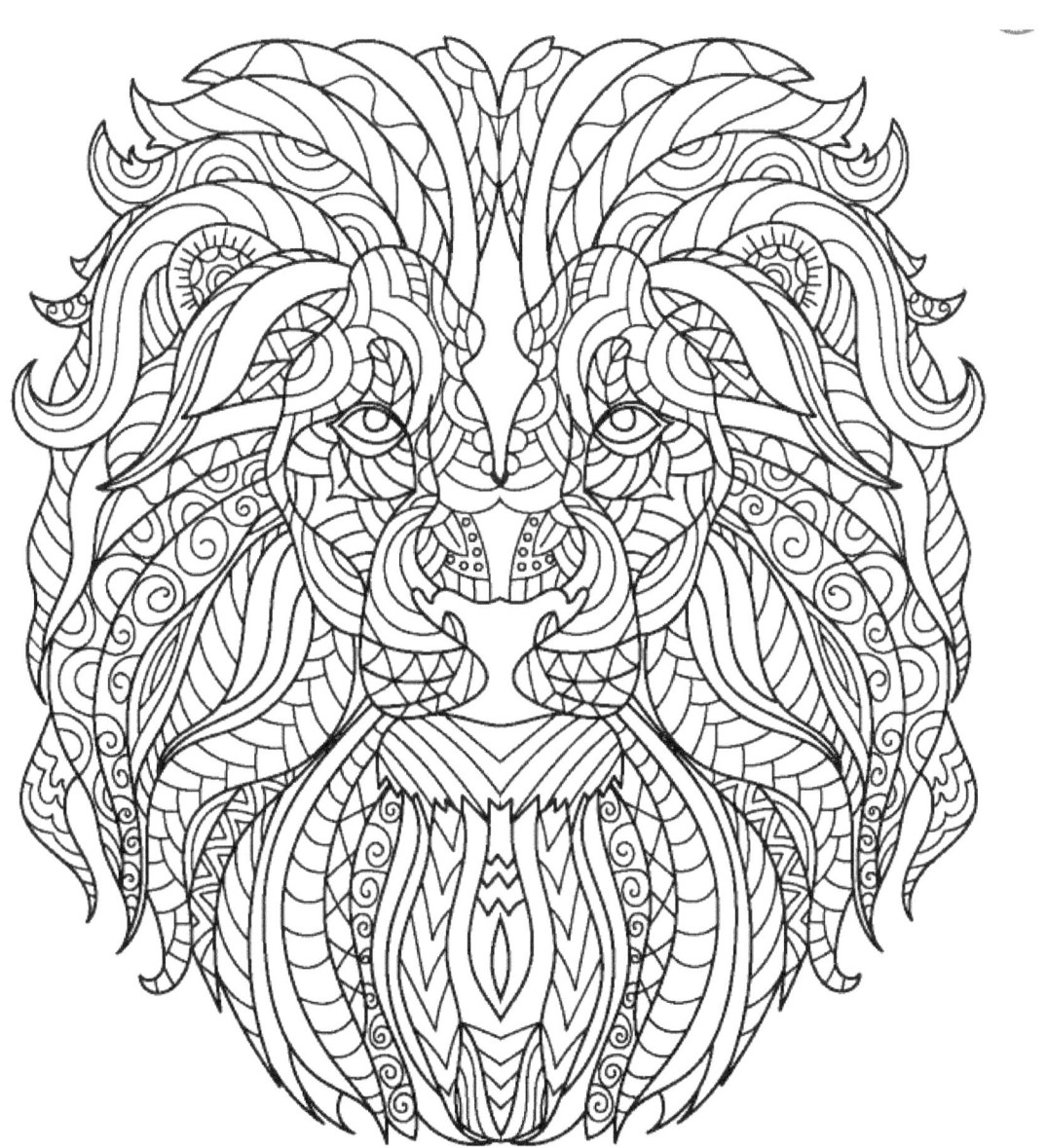

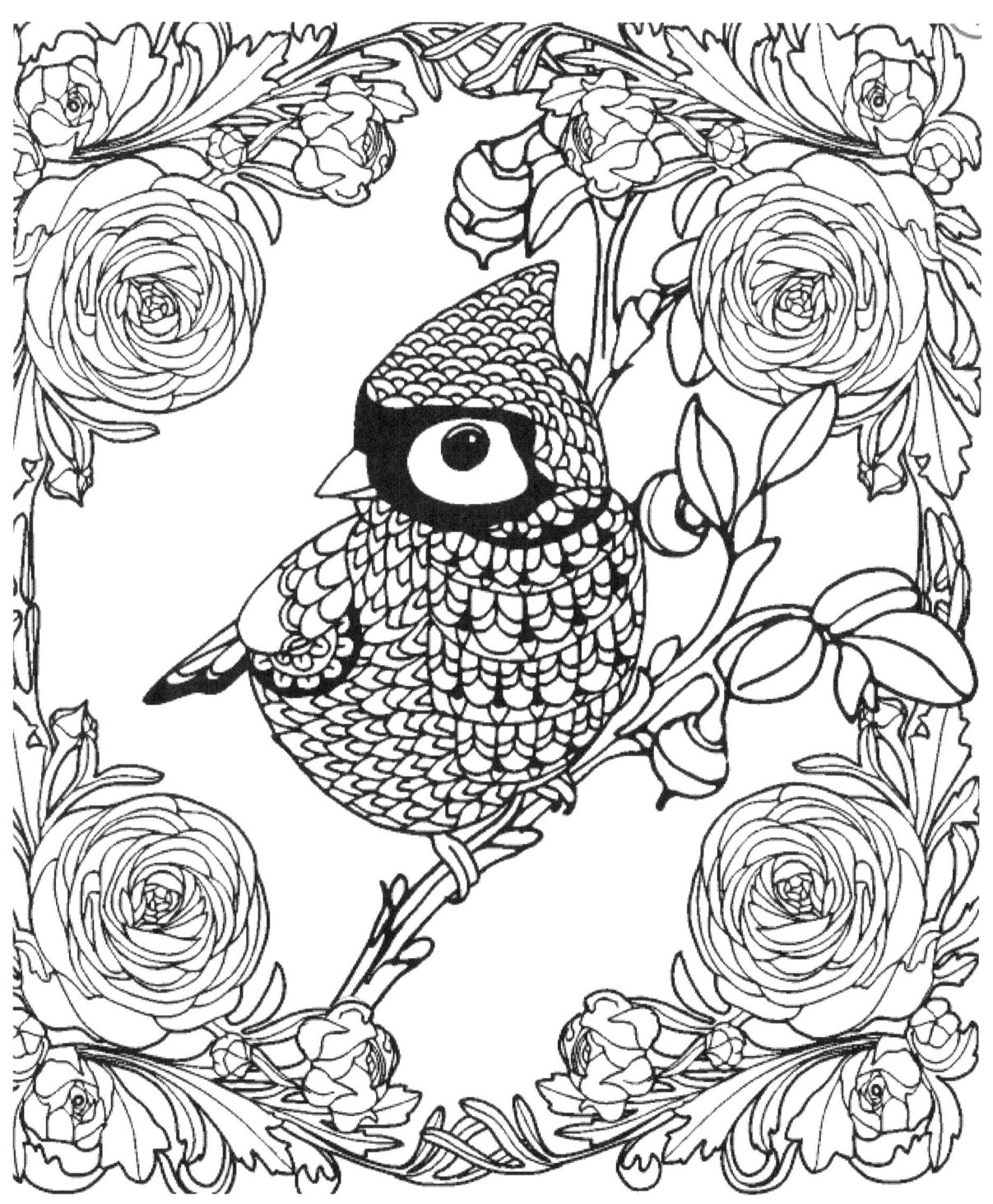

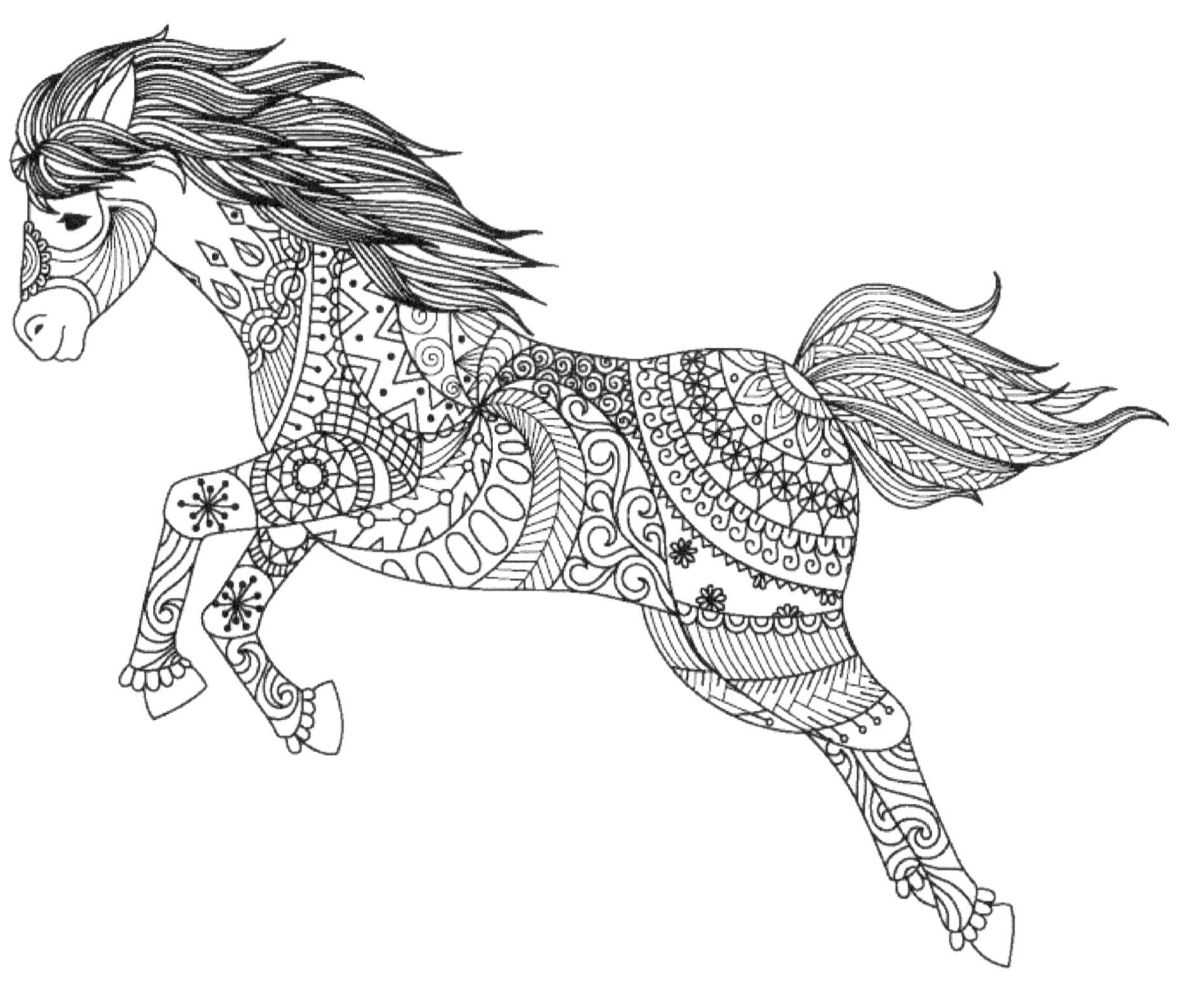

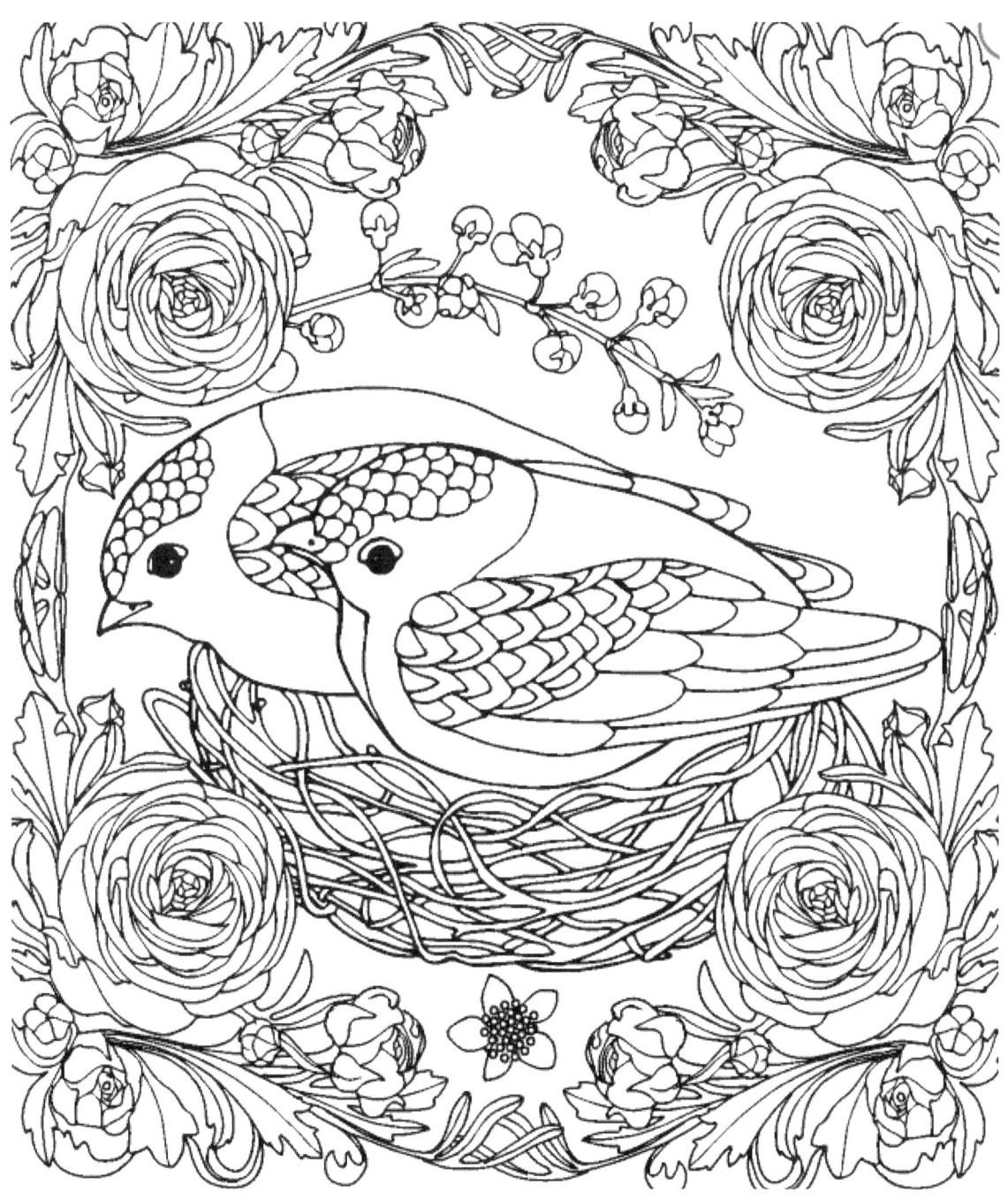

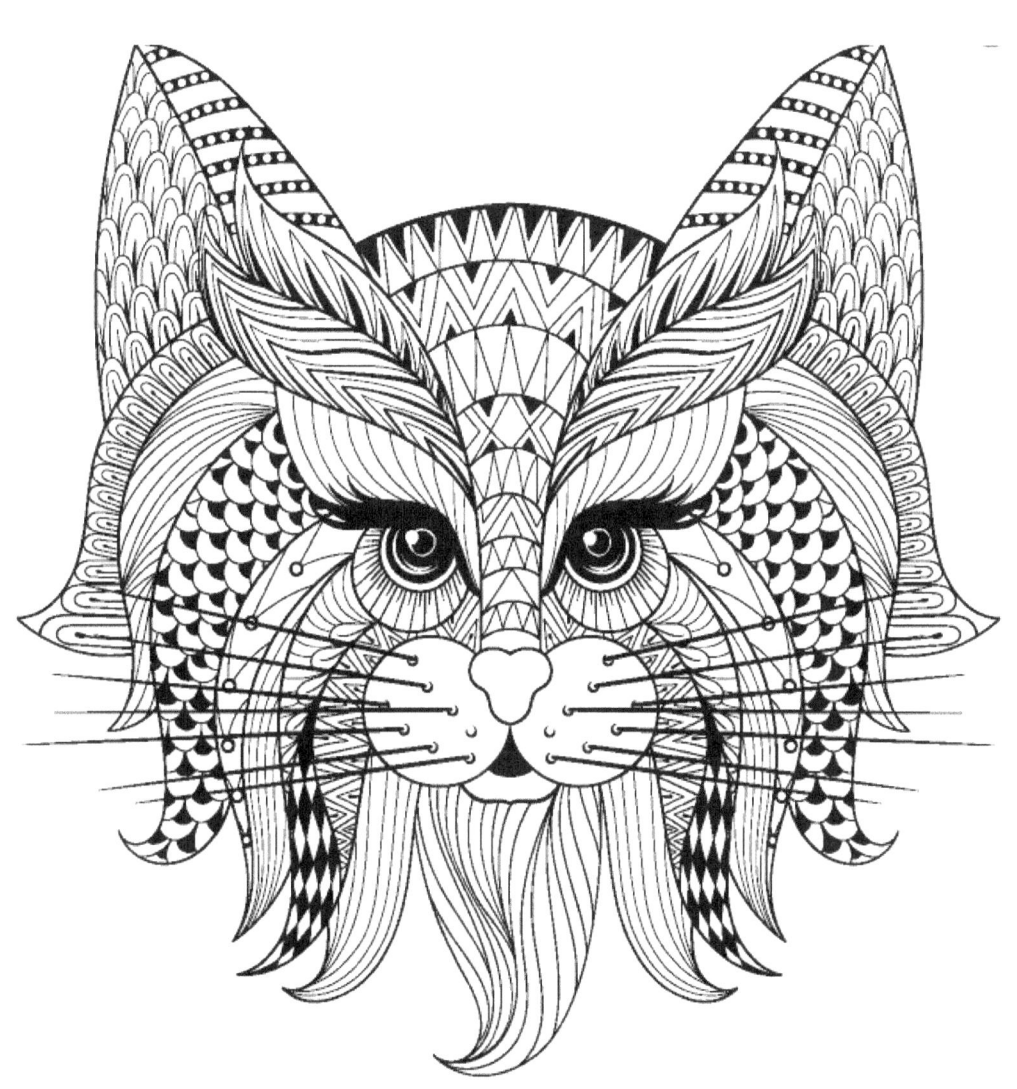

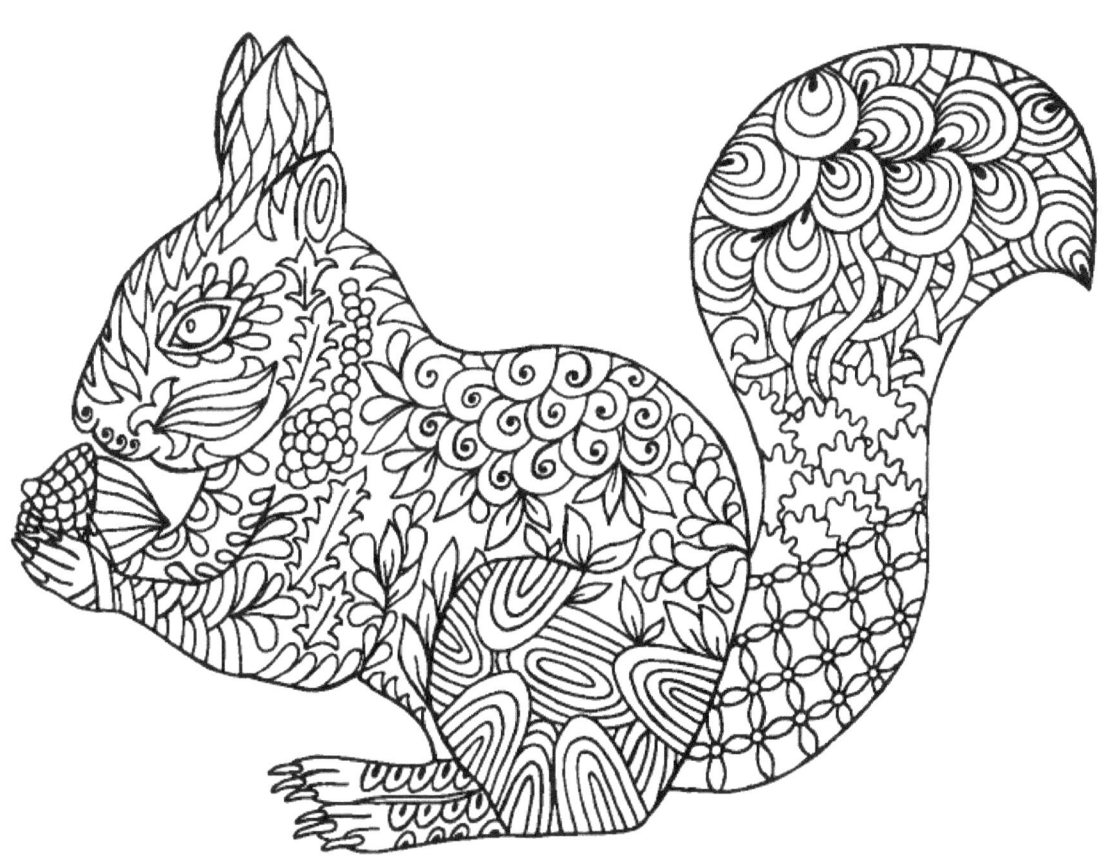

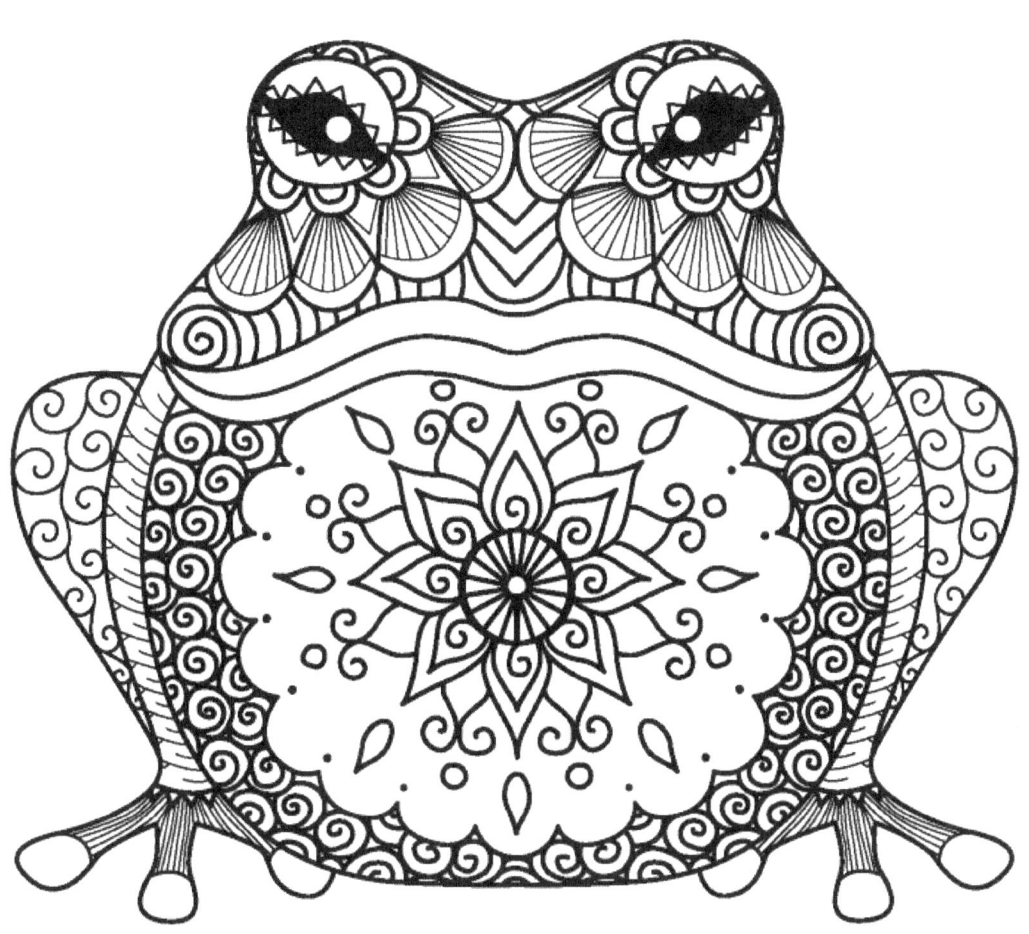

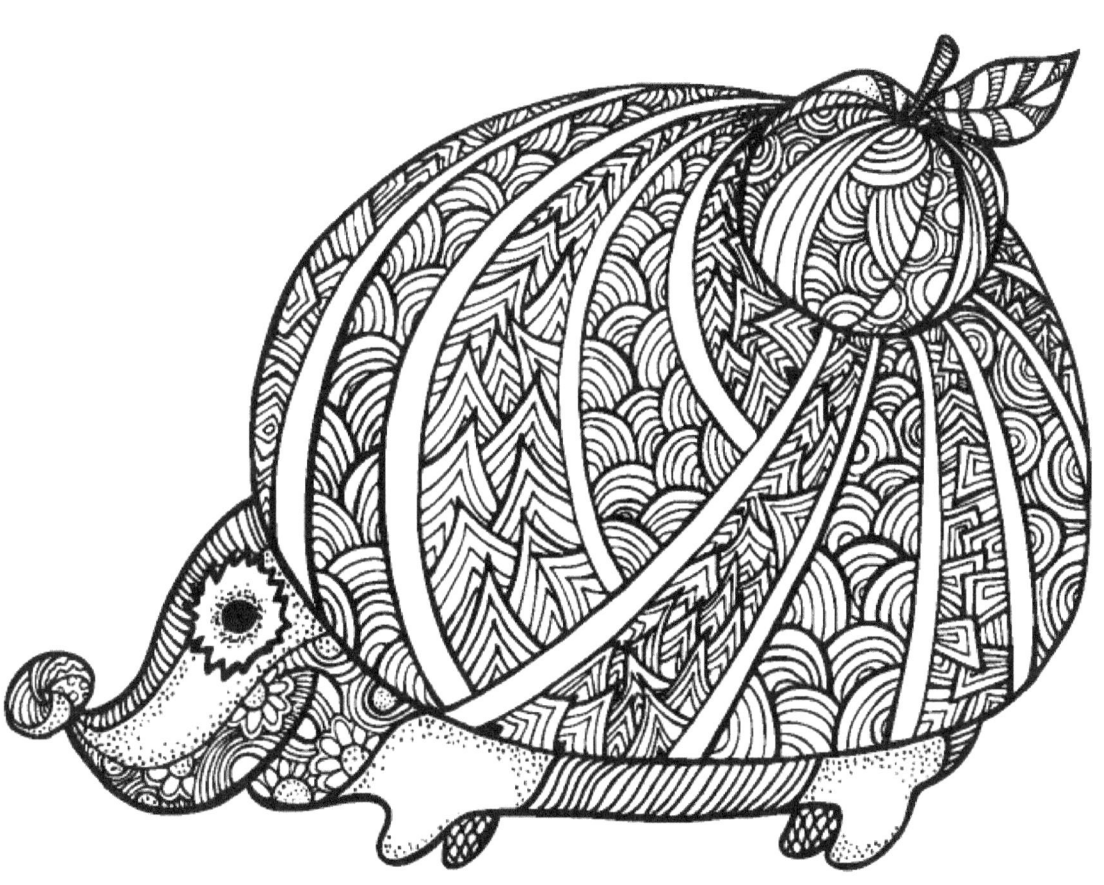

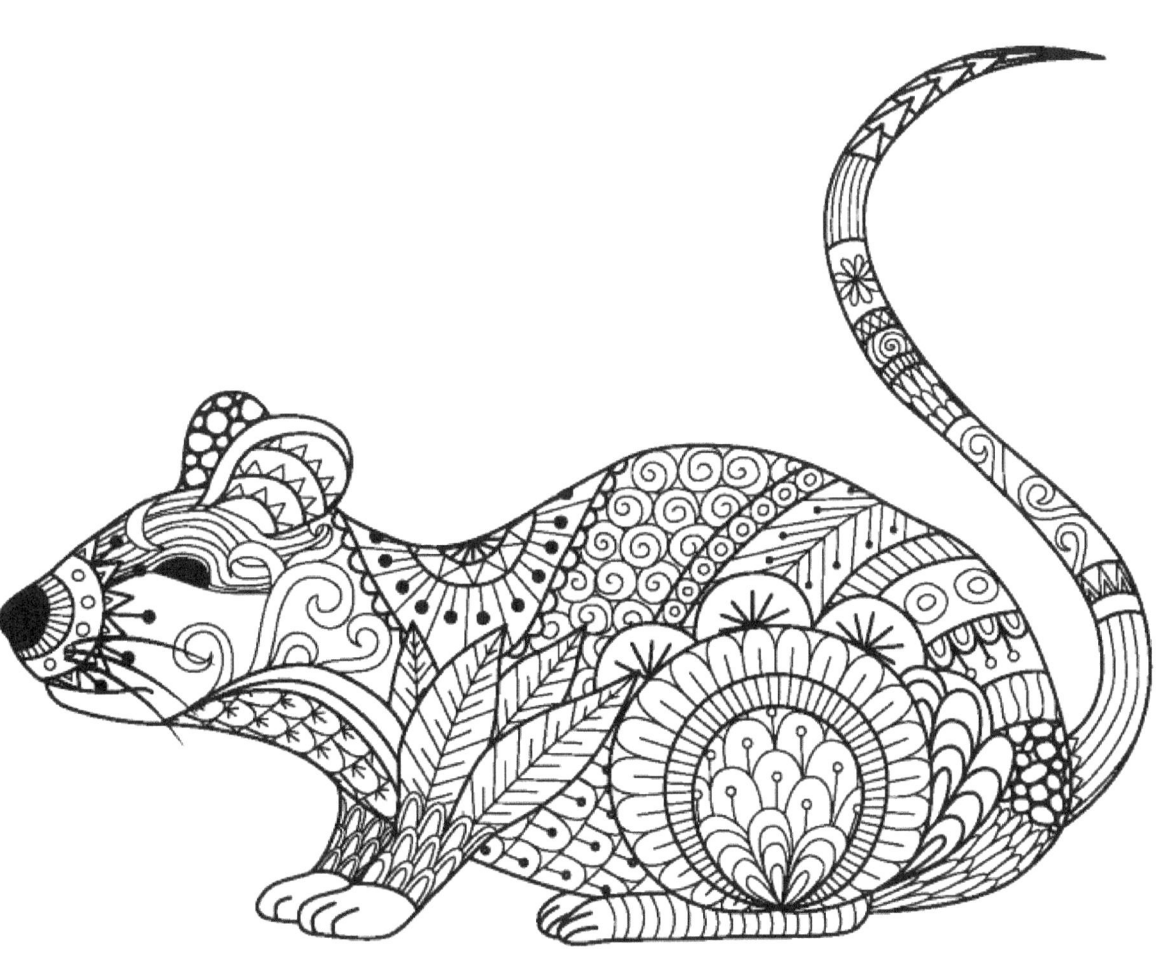

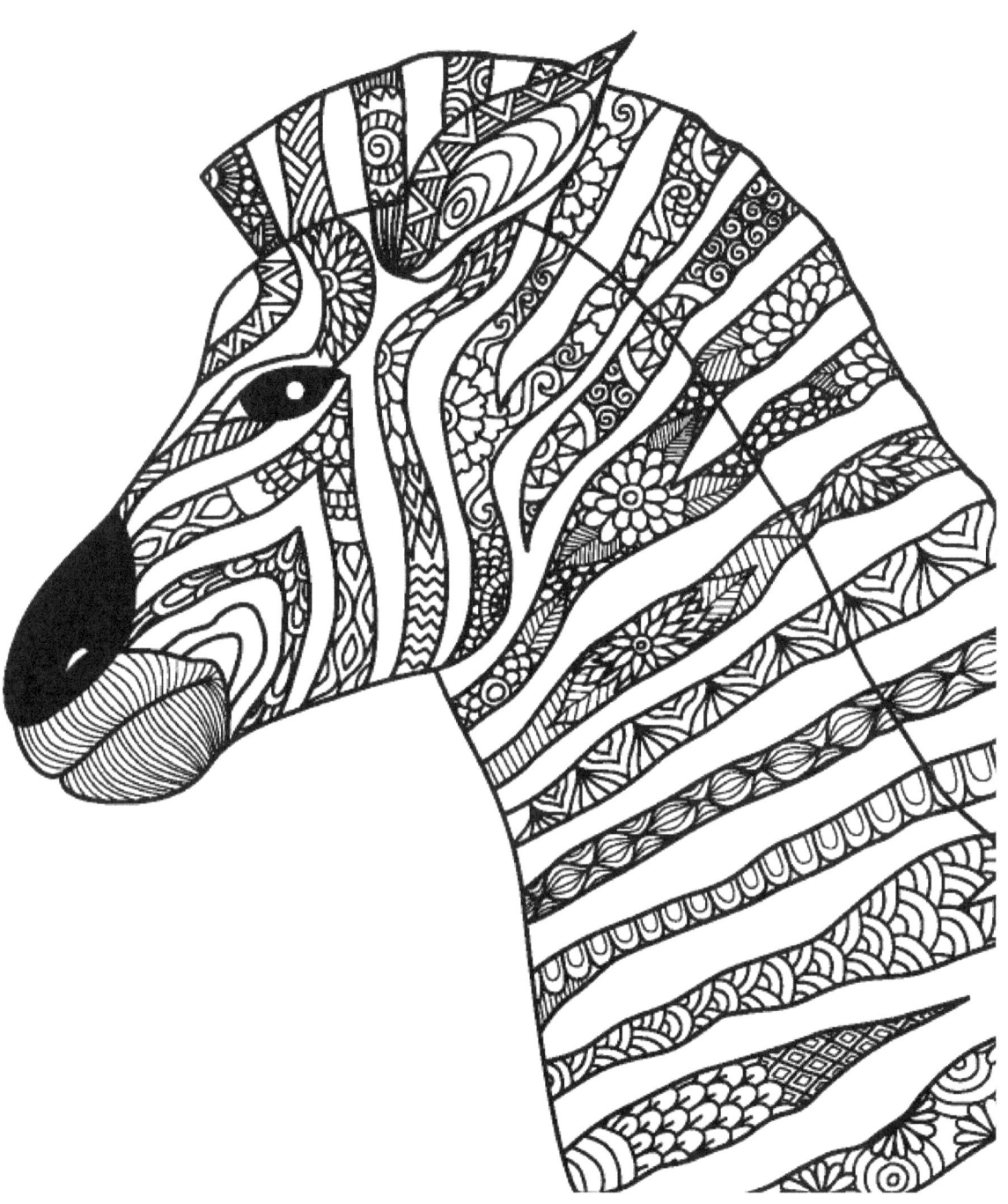

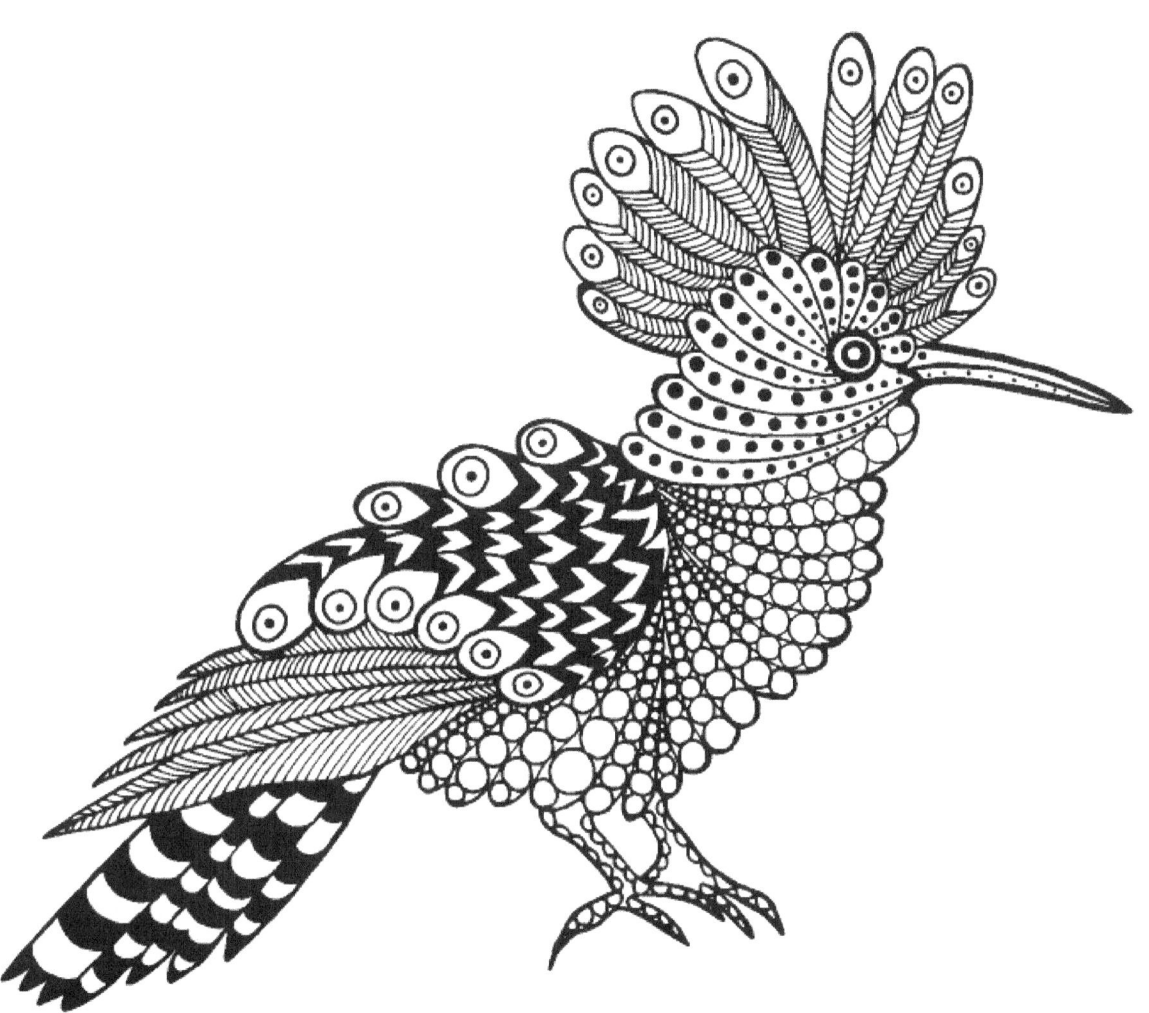

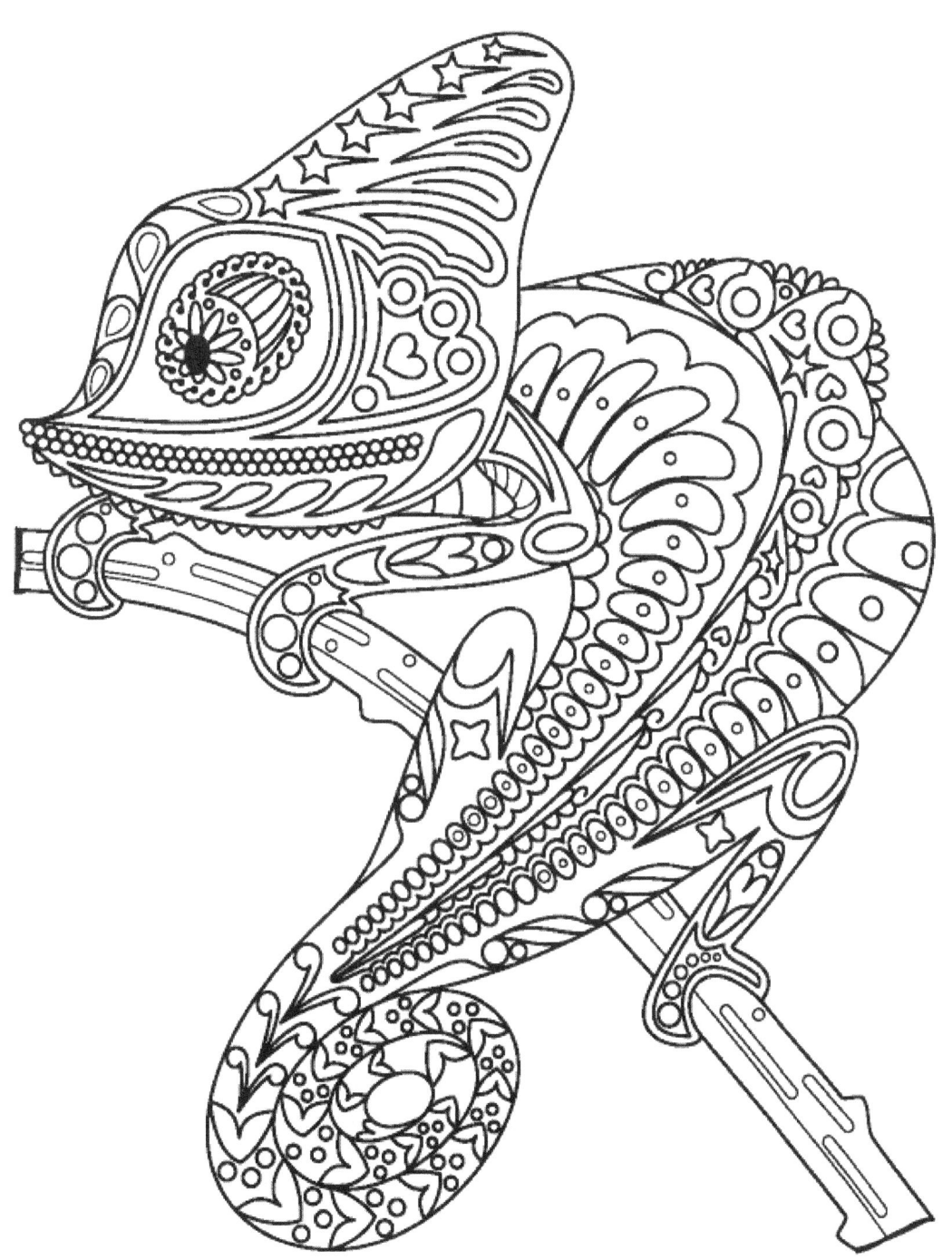

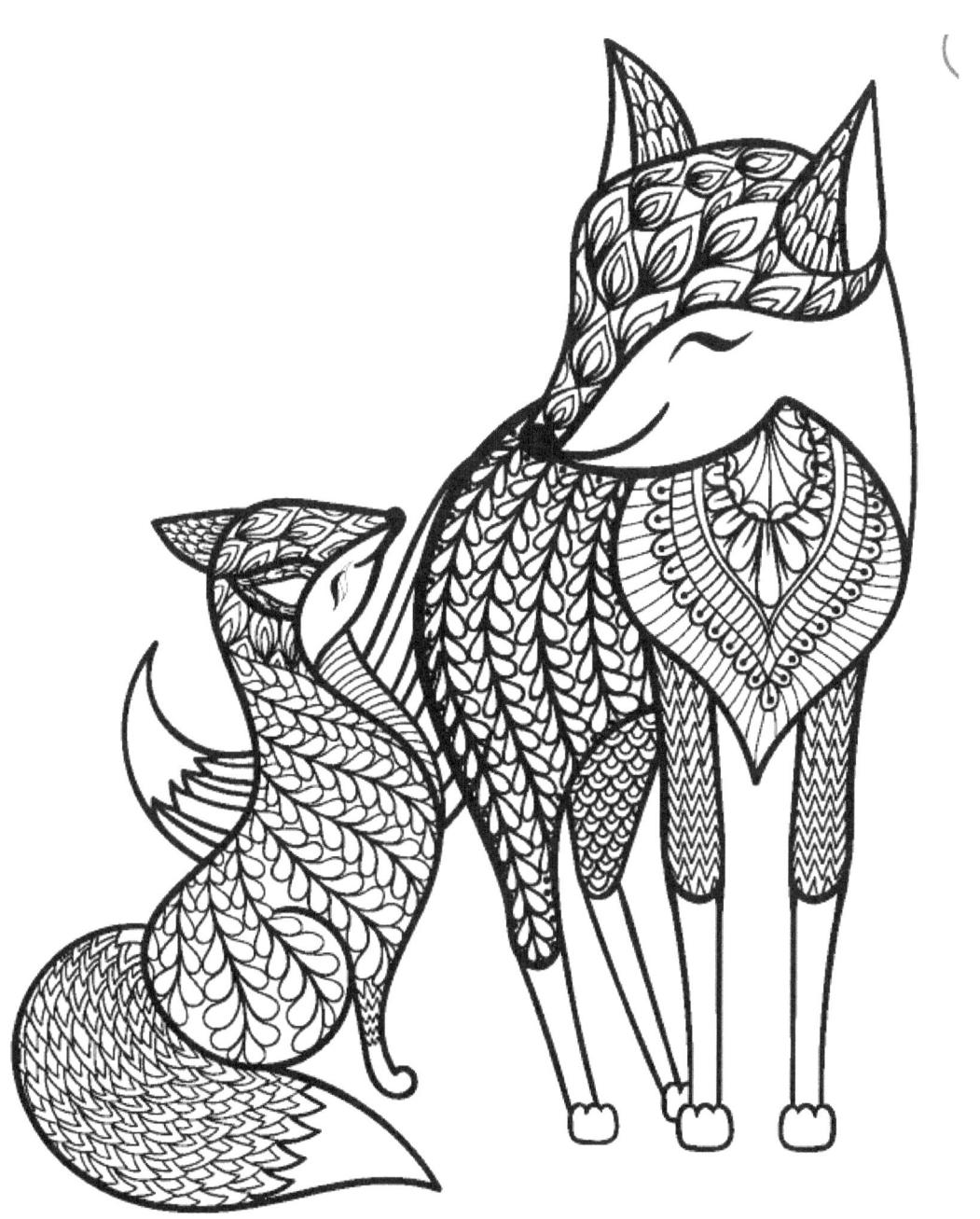

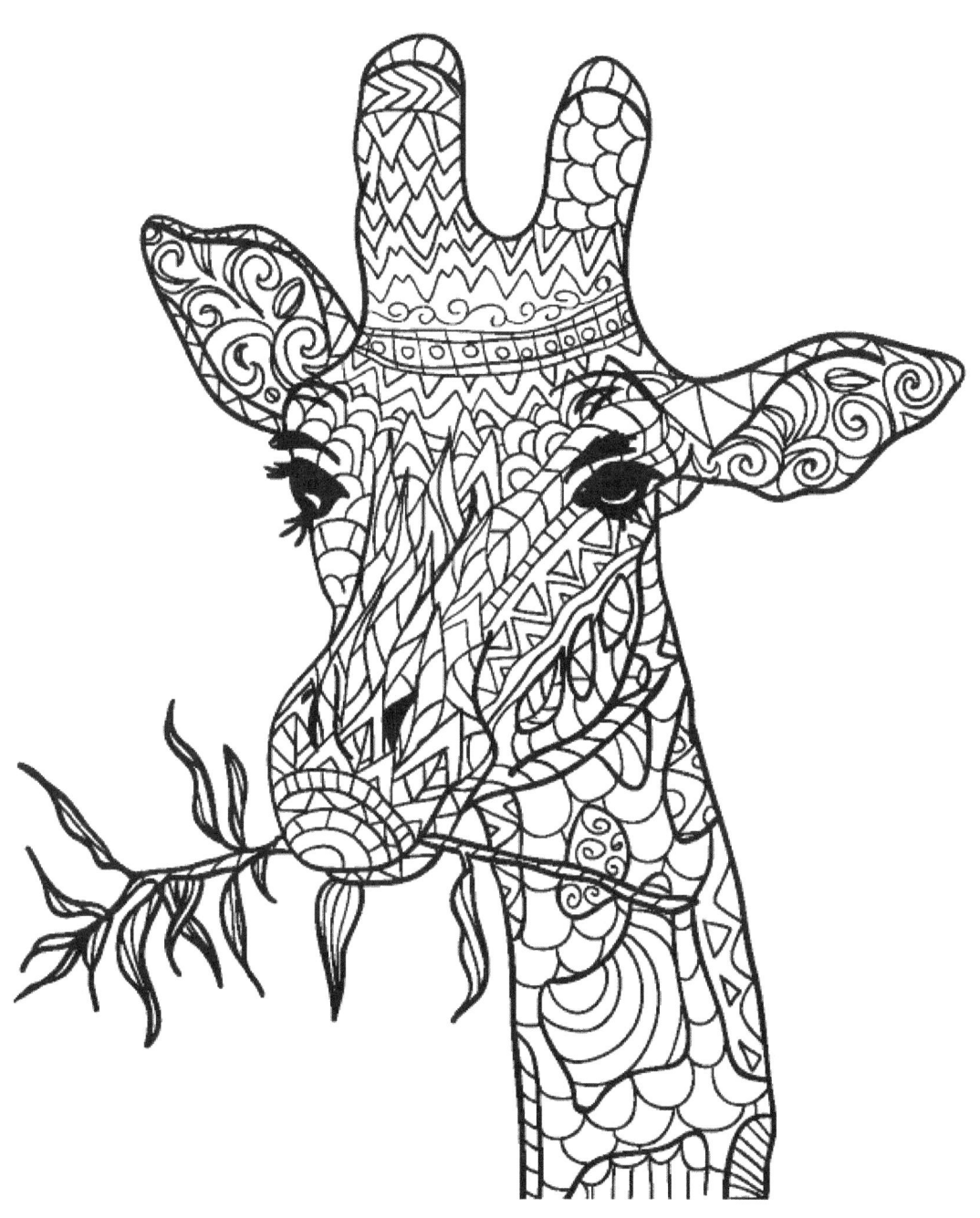

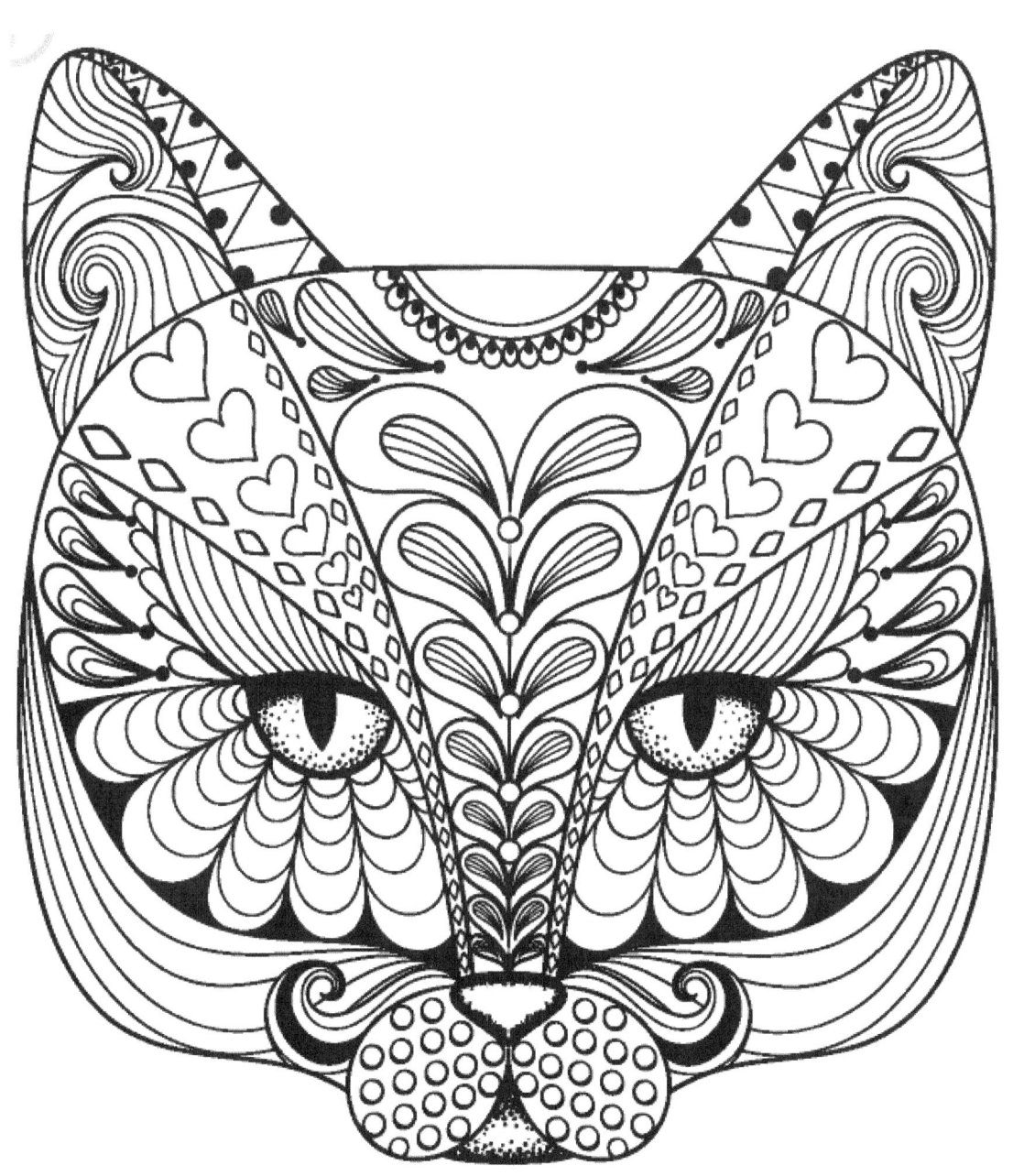

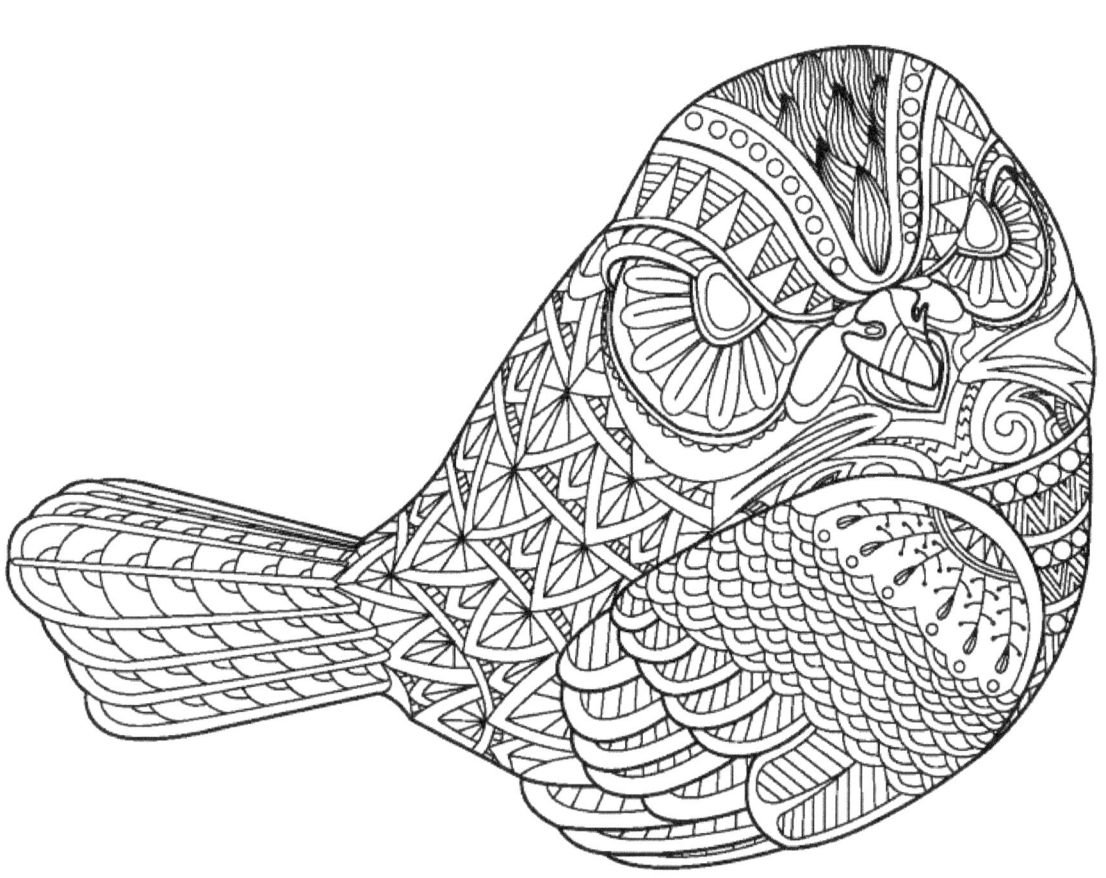

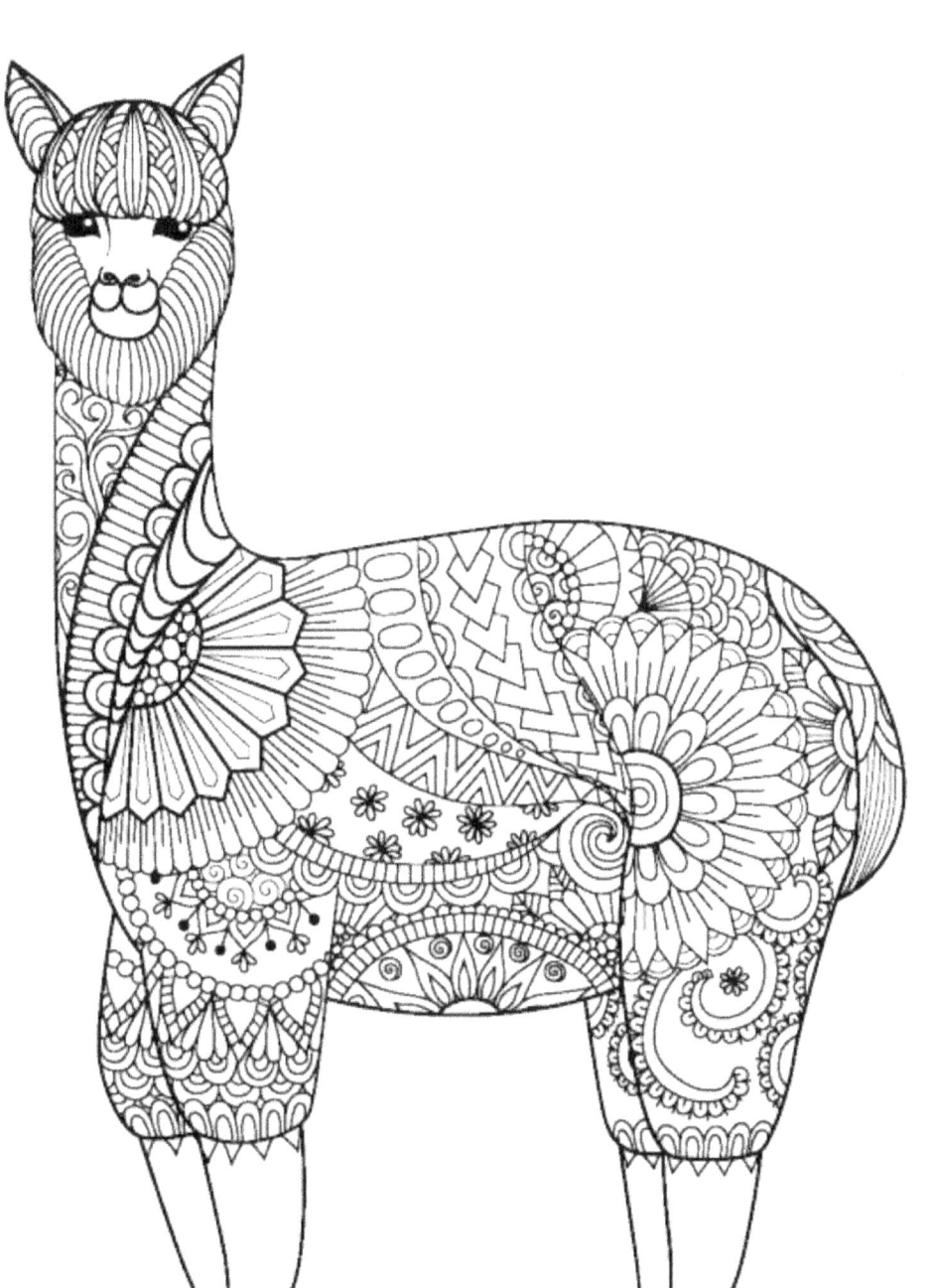

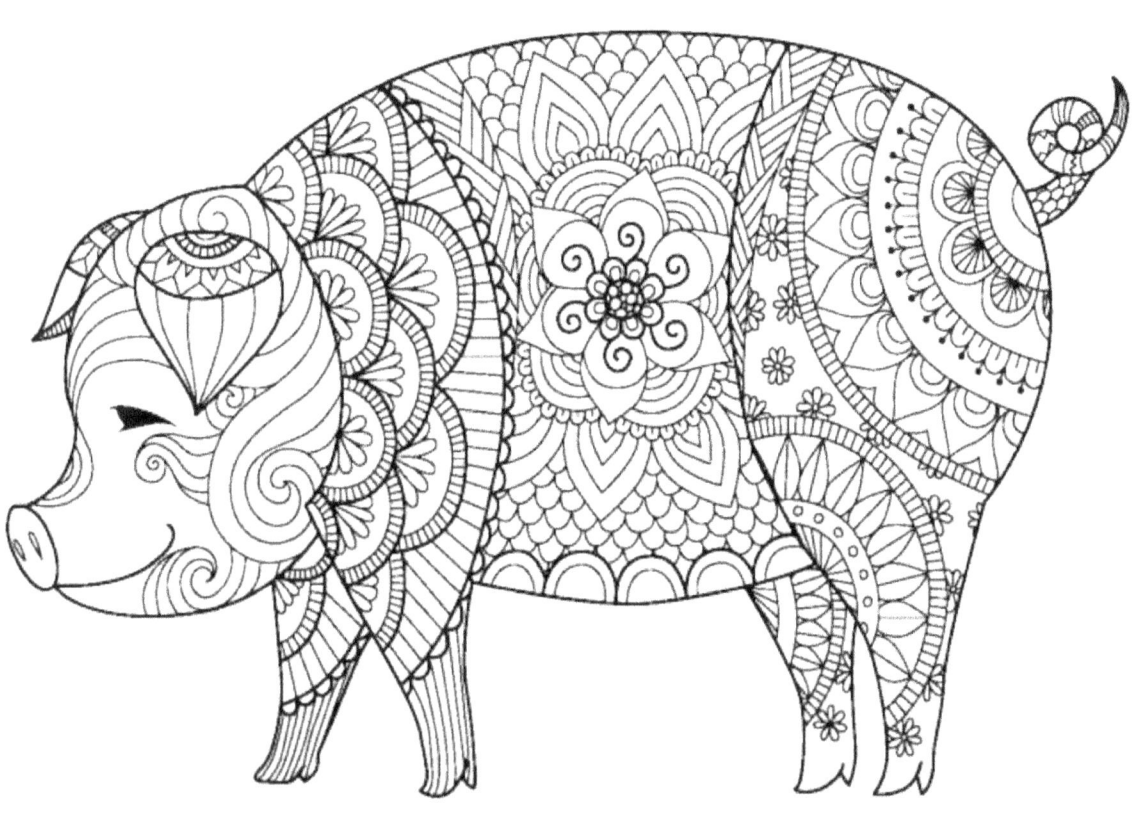

www.ingramcontent.com/pod-product-compliance
Lightning Source LLC
Chambersburg PA
CBHW060426220526
45465CB00008B/3027